The Ultimate Guide to Dog Training

How to Bring Out the Best in Your Pet

Mordecai Siegal
and Matthew Margolis

A Fireside Book
Published by Simon & Schuster

FIRESIDE
Rockefeller Center
1230 Avenue of the Americas
New York, NY 10020

First Fireside Edition 1999
FIRESIDE and colophon are registered trademarks
of Simon & Schuster Inc.
Designed by Karolina Harris
Manufactured in the United States of America
10   9
The Library of Congress has cataloged the
Simon & Schuster edition as follows:
Siegal, Mordecai.
Uncle Matty's ultimate guide to dog training / Mordecai Siegal
and Matthew Margolis.
p.   cm.
Based on the television series Woof! it's a dog's life with Matthew
Margolis.
1. Dogs—Training. I. Margolis, Matthew. II. Woof! (Television
program) III. Title.
SF431.S55   1998
636.7'088'7—dc21   98-44300 CIP
ISBN 0-684-84556-3
ISBN 0-684-85646-8 (Pbk)
National corporate sponsorship for *Woof! It's a Dog's Life* is generously
provided by Advantage® flea control.

Previously published as *Uncle Matty's Ultimate Guide to Dog Training*.

Acknowledgments

Mordecai Siegal wishes to acknowledge those whose friendship and encouragement made it possible for him to see this project through to the finish, and to retain his sanity and self-esteem during a most tumultuous time. He will always be grateful to Uncle Matty in Los Angeles; to Carol Benjamin and Stephen Lennard down the block; and most especially to Frank A., Ruth S., David Teitel, David Robert Miller, and Dave Abramowitz, who are often seen in the window at Woody's.

Matthew and Mordecai are especially grateful to their editor, Betsy Radin, whose support and consistent belief made this book possible. And thanks also to her assistant, Matt Walker.

And a very special appreciation for the best literary agent anywhere, Mel Berger, standing tall at William Morris, which is not easy to do considering the average height there.

Many thanks to Diane D'Angelo of the National Institute of Dog Training for her help and good cheer.

And we can never stop being grateful and overawed by PBS producer Laurie Donnelly of WGBH in Boston and the entire WGBH production crew who created and made happen *Woof! It's a Dog's Life with Matthew Margolis.* They're the greatest.

The least I can do is dedicate this book to my dear friend and partner, Mordecai Siegal, who made the ultimate sacrifice of becoming me for a few months. He crawled inside my mind, which he claims is like the kitchen at Burger King on a Saturday night, to write this book as if he were me. Is he Uncle Matty? Is he Uncle Morty? Is he Mordecai Siegal? No one knows. He is, now and forever, all three. God help him. He is also my very dear friend. At this moment he is busy separating tissues and marveling how you get two from one.

—Matthew Margolis

Contents

a leash correction. Leash corrections for dogs of different temperaments.

Four • Be Seated   118

How to teach your dog the command **Sit**. Four different approaches to **Sit:** the Pushing Technique; the Placing Technique; the Food Technique; and the Small-Dog Technique. **Sit** for dogs of different temperaments.

Five • Walk This Way   144

How to teach your dog the command **Heel**. Walking a Shy dog. Negotiating a new leash. Jumping while teaching **Heel**. Wrapping himself around your legs. Walking in toward you. **Heel** for dogs of different temperaments. How to teach your dog the Automatic Sit.

Six • *Stay a* While   177

Sitting and **Staying**. How to teach your dog **Stay**. The verbal command. The hand signal. Turning on your left foot. Backing off. Walking around each side of the dog. Walking around the dog. Alone in a room. **Sit-Stay** for dogs of different temperaments.

Seven • Common *Down*   208

Going **Down** and **Staying Down**. How to teach your dog the command **Down**. 1. The Hand Method. 2. The Dog's Leg Method. 3. The Push Method. 4. The Shoulder Method. 5. The Sliding-Leash Method. 6. The Foot-Leash Method. 7. The Small-Dog Method. 8. The Treat Method. Saying **Down** properly. Leash Control. Praise. The hand signal at the dog's side. Giving the hand signal while kneeling in front of the dog. **Down** without kneeling. **Down** from a greater distance. **Down** for dogs of different temperaments. How to teach your dog **Down-Stay.**

How to teach your dog the command **Come When Called** On-Leash. Gently pull the leash. Teaching the hand signal. The **Sit** position. **Come When Called** for dogs of different temperaments.

A Note to the Reader on Housebreaking Your Dog

The Ultimate Guide to Dog Training is about obedience training the way I do it on my PBS television show, *Woof! It's a Dog's Life*. It covers the essential commands for gaining control over your best buddy. In the strictest sense, housebreaking is not a part of obedience training and is not included in the lesson plan of this book. But hey, who wants to live with a dog that's going to the bathroom all over the house? There is no reason why you can't housebreak your dog at the same time you use this obedience course to train him. As a mercy for those readers who need it, I'd like to offer you my essential, no-fault method for housebreaking. Think of it as a bonus. It's okay to housebreak your dog as you use the obedience-training program in the chapters ahead.

In all my years as a dog trainer the thing that bothers dog owners the most is the poo-poo, ca-ca, wee-wee problem. I hear it all the time, all day long. I'm talking housebreaking, here. Remember that there is no such thing as a partially housebroken dog. Is he or isn't he? You only have to look at the floor for your answer. First, let's say what it is. Housebreaking is teaching your dog to go to the bathroom outside. And while we're at it, let's also define paper training. Paper training is teaching your dog to go to the bathroom in the bathroom, or on the floor in some other part of your house such as the kitchen or the basement.

Nobody wants his or her dog's "presents," "gifts," or "surprises" floating in the middle of a little yellow lagoon on the living-room floor. I believe you must either paper train your dog, on the floor inside your home, or housebreak your dog, which means teaching him to go outside. It's just too confusing for a dog to be expected to do both. Personally, I prefer housebreaking because it teaches dogs to never use the floor as a toilet, with or without paper.

Some dogs are harder to housebreak than others. I can't explain it so don't ask me why.

One of my clients once said, "My dog makes little spite pees."

"Spite pees?" I asked.

"Yes. I take her out, I walk her, I do everything right, I come back and give her some quality playtime and what does she do? She walks right over to me and pees on my feet. And that's after she did everything outside. Go figure. I don't know where it all comes from."

I'd like to offer you my five-part method for housebreaking:

1. Diet
2. Confining the dog.
3. Proper correction.
4. Getting rid of the odor.
5. Feeding and walking schedule.

Diet

The first consideration is what to feed the dog. I suggest you do not feed him different foods at scattered times while you're housebreaking him. When housebreaking a puppy or an adult dog it is essential that you get him on a diet that is appropriate for his age and lifestyle. Do not feed your dog leftovers from your dinner table, especially while he is being housebroken. A dinner of leftovers, no matter how large or good, does not guarantee that the dog is getting all the nutrition he needs. Most important of all, it does not work well with the feeding schedule that is such an important part of this training method. Inadequate diet, irregular feeding, snacks between meals, and sudden changes of food all work against the training. Every one of these factors can cause a digestion problem such as diarrhea during housebreaking and make it impossible to complete the training.

Select any high-quality, premium dog food and feed your dog that one product, at least until he's housebroken. It's good for him. It's formulated for him. It's consistent. It won't upset his stomach, and it definitely won't upset the schedule.

Confining the dog.

The second thing to do is confine your dog if you are not home to watch him. If you give him the run of the house while you're trying to housebreak him, you will never get the job done. If you can't keep a sharp eye on the dog and look for the signs that he has to go, then you must confine him to one small location inside your house. The best way to do this is with a dog crate. A crate is a wire cage with a little door at the front and a solid bottom that confines the dog in one place. Some people do not like crates because they think it's a sort of prison. I don't think it's a prison; I think it's a condo. If you put in a little carpeting, a lamp, a VCR, a TV, and a fridge, it's wonderful.

Seriously, crates don't make the puppy feel bad. It's like a cave or a den, which is exactly what dogs create for themselves in the wild. Just put a soft blanket or towel in the crate along with some toys and your pet will adjust to it quickly. Big dogs need a big crate and small dogs need a small crate. The crate should be large enough for the dog to stand up and move around a bit, but do not make it too large or it loses its den-like quality. You can confine a dog in a crate for four or five hours at a time, no more. Every time you let the dog out of the crate you must walk him so he can relieve himself. This is all about a dog's natural denning instinct, where he creates a place he can sleep in peace. Dogs generally do not soil their den or crate unless they cannot help themselves.

If you don't like a crate or you don't have room for one, confine the dog in the kitchen with a puppy gate, the kind you get in a hardware store. Until the dog is housebroken, confine his movements in the house to one small room when no one is home. When you let him out of the confined area, watch him closely for signs that he wants to go. The usual area of confinement is the kitchen because of its convenience and because the floor there is covered with linoleum. Always use a see-through puppy gate to confine your dog so he doesn't feel imprisoned or isolated. That would be the worst thing you could do to a dog, which is the most social of all animals.

Proper correction.

Do not punish your dog if he has an accident. If you catch him in the act, say *No* in a very firm tone of voice, praise him, and rush him outdoors to his toilet area and praise him lavishly if he uses it. You can also shake an empty soda can with ten pennies inside and use that as a correction device. Shake the can and say *No* if the dog is urinating on the floor. Do not do this once the dog has already made the mistake. A minute or two after he makes his mistake, your dog has no idea what he is being corrected for. You must take him outdoors and encourage him to go again and praise him for it.

Under no circumstances should you ever hit your dog or rub his nose in his own mess. You may feel better, but it only teaches your dog to fear you and has nothing to do with teaching housebreaking. Fear is not a good basis for a loving relationship or for teaching anything. Instead, you must communicate to your dog that he did something wrong. This can be accomplished with a leash correction, a verbal correction such as *No* spoken in a loud, firm voice, or a noise correction with a shaken soda can with pennies in it. All corrections must be followed immediately with verbal praise so the dog feels rewarded for having stopped his misbehavior. It also tells him that you are not mad at him.

Ideally, a dog should be stopped in the middle of making a mistake with a correction, but it is only effective if you catch him in the act. If you do, say *No* in a firm tone of voice. At the same time, jerk the leash, if he is wearing one, or vigorously rattle the soda can if it is available. Praise the dog and run him out to the place where he is permitted to relieve himself.

It is essential that you consider your dog's temperament when correcting him. If the noise from the soda can is too loud or *No* is said too harshly, you could scare a Shy dog and have the opposite effect that you want. You should never use a noise correction for a Shy dog, especially if it makes him cower with fear. Correct dogs of that temperament with a soft tone of voice. A Stubborn or High-Energy dog requires a vigorous correction with a loud, firm tone of voice. An Easygoing or Sedate dog requires a medium-firm tone of voice and no noise corrections with the soda can. Most other type dogs simply require a firm *No* and a vigorous rattle of the soda can or a jerk of the leash if he has it on.

Getting rid of the odor.

You must get rid of the odor of your dog's accidents. This is very important. Dogs are always drawn back to the same spot they soiled, and they can smell it long after you have scrubbed it away and it seems to be gone. The only sure way to get rid of the odor is with an odor neutralizer available in pet-supply stores and mail-order pet catalogs. These work best.

It is normal for dogs to scent post or establish their territory with urine and feces. Once they do this, they are continually drawn back to the same places outdoors or indoors to relieve themselves right on top of the other scent markers. Even when you cannot smell the exact location, he can. His incredible sense of smell combines with his instinct to mark territory and to keep marking it over and over again. To break the cycle in your home, you must obliterate those undetectable odors. Commercial cleaning products will not eliminate the scent. Incidentally, liquid ammonia is the worst thing you can use because it simulates the basic ingredient of urine.

Feeding and walking schedule.

Scheduling has to do with when you feed and water your dog in relation to when you walk him. This is very important. You need to attend to a puppy every three to four hours and get him outside that often. In other words, when you get up in the morning, take him out. Come back inside, feed and water him, and take him out again, right away. Do this three times over the next eight to ten hours. Older dogs must be fed and watered less frequently but need just as many walks. See the schedule at the end of this section.

Feed and water your dog on a consistent schedule so his need to eliminate will also be on a consistent schedule. Giving a dog water all day long is a mistake for housebreaking. If you give your dog water all day while housebreaking him, he's going to drink and urinate all day. If you schedule his water intake for every four or five hours, you won't have that problem. The same is true for between-meal snacks. Do not feed your dog anything except his regularly scheduled meals. The idea of the chart that follows is to create a body clock within your dog so he will relieve himself at those scheduled times and only then, no matter what. Consistency is the key to success with this method. Follow the chart below until you feel your dog has the hang of things. Of course, these schedules are only for the time that you are housebreaking your dog, which could last anywhere between two to four weeks or two to four months, depending on the dog. Some dogs make the adjustment in less than a week, but that is rare.

Schedule for Puppies Seven Weeks to Six Months Old*

7 A.M.   Walk the dog.
7:30 A.M.   Feed, water, and walk.

11:30 A.M.   Feed, water, and walk.
4:30 P.M.   Feed, water, and walk.
8:30 P.M.   Water and walk (last water of the day).
11:30 P.M.   Walk the dog.

Schedule for Puppies Six to Twelve Months Old*

7 A.M.   Walk the dog.
7:30 A.M.   Feed, water, and walk.
12:30 P.M.   Water and walk.
4:30 P.M.   Feed, water, and walk.
7:30 P.M.   Water and walk (last water of the day).
11 P.M.   Walk the dog.

Schedule for Dogs Twelve Months and Older*

7 A.M.   Walk the dog.
7:30 A.M.   Feed, water, and walk.
4:30 P.M.   Feed, water, and walk.
7:30 P.M.   Water and walk (last water of the day).
11 P.M.   Walk the dog.

Schedule for Working People*

Before leaving for work   Feed, water, and walk the
                            dog.
Midday   If possible, have a friend,
                            relative, neighbor, or hired
                            person feed, water, and

	walk your puppy. (Only water and a walk for an adult dog.)
Home from work	Walk the dog.
Early evening	Feed, water and walk the dog (last water of the day).
Before bedtime	Walk the dog.

*Consult your vet about feeding your dog or puppy.

When you are at work, keep the dog confined in a designated area with a see-through puppy gate. Do not place newspaper on the floor. Expect accidents. Clean them up when you come home and do not correct the dog for them. You may use a wire dog crate, providing someone comes in to walk the dog at midday.

Introduction

Curling up with an enjoyable companion book has many of the same benefits as curling up with an enjoyable companion animal. The difference between the two is merely a tail. It has been proved that petting a friendly dog can reduce tension and lower pulse rate. The same can be said of a user-friendly book, and in particular, a companion book to a popular television show. *The Ultimate Guide to Dog Training* was written to complement and amplify the fun and highly useful dog training information found in every segment of the television series *Woof! It's a Dog's Life with Matthew Margolis.* This entertaining television series is now seen throughout the United States and in many parts of the world. Presented on PBS by WGBH Boston, Matthew has become known to his vast TV audience as Uncle Matty, a *nom de pooch* that has become permanently stamped into the minds of the dog-owning public. It began in a casual, spontaneous way. Whenever one of his tail-wagging students performed a command properly, Matthew rewarded the dog with exuberant praise and affection. He would say in a high-pitched tone of voice, "Oh, my dog. Uncle Matty's *so* proud!" Everyone watching fell in love with the way he praised the dogs and the animals' exhilarated response to him. Matthew has since become America's dog trainer—and to his affectionate audience, he will forever be Uncle Matty.

Although *The Ultimate Guide to Dog Training* is a dog-training book, it is not like any other. Of course, it presents expert obedience training for dogs and dog lovers. If you read it, you will learn. However, the instructions offered in this book are given within the framework of scenarios between the dog, Matthew, and the dog's owners, as is done in the television series. All the essentials of dog training are here—including bonding, training equipment and commands, all bundled into an effective obedience program for you and your dog. But there is one big difference between this book and other training manuals. We have added an important character that usually never appears in this type of book, the person who has to do the work, the dog's owner—meaning you. Before you can teach your dog obedience training *you* must learn how to do it first. Every dog-training book by necessity is about teaching people how to train their dogs. For that reason we have included dog owners in each scenario so they can reveal the things that hold them back from doing a good job. In some instances, the stumbling blocks are quite humorous. In other cases, they are somewhat serious. You may be surprised to find unexpected laughter and perhaps a tear or two in the pages of this dog-training book. We want to make it easier and more enjoyable to train your dog. It will certainly be more interesting.

Each chapter teaches a specific aspect of obedience training, with different dogs and their owners, and is performed in lively scenes with all the players involved. Within training scenes, we occasionally find that the dog and its owner have an identity crisis, so we try to figure out who is on which end of the leash. In this book, the four-legged family members and the folks who love them will make you laugh, or grumble, or, perhaps wince with recognition.

The Ultimate Guide to Dog Training is the collaboration between two men who have been writing dog books together for three decades; the words are by Mordecai Siegal and the music by Matthew Margolis. Mordecai has written twenty-three books, sixteen of them about dogs, and Uncle Matty, *so proud,* has trained more than 35,000 dogs. This collaboration began in 1969 and has resulted in eight books, several of which are among the most successful dog books in print.

"Uncle Matty" Margolis has made an unforgettable impression on everyone who watches him on TV. Millions of viewers enjoy Matthew's television shows because the dog owners as well as their dogs often trip over themselves, doing everything wrong, revealing what they'll do for love, and finally, learning how to succeed in training without really crying. The concept of owner participation is reflected on these pages, along with step-by-step teaching techniques that really work. All that's missing is the falsetto sound of Matthew squealing to adoring dogs. If you have ever watched him on television, then you are familiar with this high-pitched sound of exhilaration, enchanting the dogs he trains along with their owners.

Matthew's one-hour specials continue to help PBS stations across the country with their membership pledge drives, and he endears himself to everyone who watches him change the behavior of dogs before their eyes. Of equal importance is Uncle Matty's understanding of humans in relation to their pets. His funny manner in pointing out the mistakes people make with their dogs is not only entertaining, it is an important part of the instruction. The people who appear on the shows with their dogs, and everyone watching at home, are enriched by the experience. As a result, everyone on the show and at home watching comes away with a better understanding of their dogs and the world they inhabit, how to manage behavior problems, and how to love their dogs more openly. It is the presence of the owners and their dogs that makes the TV specials so special. Having the owners as well as the dogs in each training scene is what makes *The Ultimate Guide to Dog Training* a very unusual dog book. Matty and Morty are *so* proud!

One
Test Case

Ever since I began saying to my tail-wagging students on television, "Come to Uncle Matty," the name has stuck to me like dog hair in the spring. As a result, it's almost impossible to find anyone who calls me anything else. To tell the truth, I love it because wherever I go I'm treated like every dog's favorite uncle, and that's the best compliment I've ever gotten. So if you're going to train your dog with my help, just call me Uncle Matty. If you can spare a few minutes every day for the next nine to ten weeks, and if you're determined to have a well-mannered, friendly dog, I can help you train him in a way that is fun and easy.

It's a nice, sunny day today here on the beach in Southern California, and I'm standing next to Jeanette and her eight-month-old shepherd-mix, Punch, who she rescued from an animal shelter when he was six months old. Punch is a fairly large dog and seems very sweet, but if I'm going to train him, I need to know more about him. And that's the point to this chapter.

"Jeanette, hand me the leash and we'll see what we can find out. Hey guy. Say hello to Uncle Matty."

Matty squeals with delight in a high falsetto voice, as though he was talking to a baby, and affectionately cups the dog's face in his hands.

"Oh my, Uncle Matty's proud! Give me a kiss! What a sweet dog."

The dog wags his tail as he gives Matty one quick slurp on his nose with his tongue. Matty hands the leash back to Jeanette.

You can learn how to train your dog by paying attention to what I do in each training session. First things first, though. Let's talk about one of the most important steps to take before the training. It involves determining your dog's temperament. If you know your dog's temperament, you can tailor your training techniques so he'll respond properly with a minimum of problems. For example, if you have a stubborn dog, you have to be firm and persistent with your corrections but very encouraging and enthusiastic with your praise. If you have a sensitive, timid, or shy dog, you have to be gentle and reserved when correcting him, if you can correct him at all, and you must praise him lavishly for doing the right things. An aggressive dog with high energy must be handled firmly and cautiously, especially when correcting him. You must praise him in a subdued manner for executing the commands properly or he will jump around with excitement and not get trained. By paying attention to your dog's personality, you will quickly learn that his responses dictate how to handle him for the best results. This is not too hard to figure out once you get the idea. Chapter Four deals with praise and corrections in greater detail. It doesn't take a rocket scientist to understand what kind of dog you have, either. All you need to do is give him a few easy, uncomplicated tests to figure out his temperament. These simple tests also give you some clues about how quickly or slowly he's going to learn by observing how quickly he responds to you.

Before we do that, though, I'd like to say one or two things about the Uncle Matty approach to dog training, because people always ask me about it. I train dogs using love, praise, and affection. I also train them from the dog's point of view. I try to think like a dog and put myself in the animal's position. If you do the same, it will make a world of difference in how well you treat the furry member of the family. I make it my business to let the dog know that I'm his friend and that I love him and understand him. That's what Uncle Matty is about, including the high-pitched tone of voice I use at special times, which to some people sounds like baby talk.

Matthew turns to Punch, who is still being held by Jeanette, and puts his face nose to nose with him and squeals again with his baby talk, falsetto voice.

"Oh, my. Uncle Matty's proud. Hello, my Captain Punch, how are you today?"

He hugs the dog.

Your dog needs to know that you're not mad at him, no matter what he may have done, especially when he makes a mistake. I never show anger to a dog. That's because I never really get mad at him. And I would never punish him for his mistakes. You must never lose it with your dog or threaten him with a rolled-up newspaper or with accusations like "What did you do, you bad dog!" These things only destroy the bonds of friendship and trust between you and your dog, and actually make training harder. You wouldn't do that to a child, would you? I hope not. Well, your dog is like your kid, and he deserves to be treated the same way. So, what *do* you do when the dog makes a mistake or refuses to obey a command? You must teach your dog the specifics of a command, and then get him to execute them as many times as it takes for him to understand what to do. How else will he know what to do? Dog training requires communication, instruction, and repetition, but the most important part is communication of feelings, good thoughts, and of course teaching. Things almost always go well when the communication is good. Your dog really *is* your best friend, and you have to be *his* best friend. I have a teaching formula that applies to every dog. It's very simple: command, correction, and praise. When he performs properly you must praise him. When he makes a mistake you must correct him and then praise him immediately after. If you follow that formula, you will have the best dog possible and a lifetime of enjoyable friendship. That, my friends, is the Uncle Matty approach to dog training.

He turns to Jeanette who is standing next to him.

"For example, when teaching Punch the command *Sit*, tell him he's a good boy if he performs correctly. If you want him to hold his position, give him the command, *Stay*, using a hand signal that I'll teach you in Chapter Seven. If he stays, praise him enthusiastically with compliments like, 'Good Boy! What a great dog! I'm so proud of you!' Of course, if you don't teach him the specifics of these commands, there's no way for him to know what to do. In each chapter, I will teach the specifics of each command so you will know what to do."

Jeanette hugs her dog as though he was a child and kisses him on top of his head.

"Sure, sure, Matthew. It's easy for you, because you're a dog trainer. But what happens if he doesn't do it right for me? You get to be good old Uncle Matty because you can get a dog to do anything. You're a pro. But every time *I* tell Punch what to do, he just turns his head to the side and looks at me and smirks."

"He smirks?"

"You heard me, he smirks. You can actually see his lips form a smirk as he shakes his head with disapproval. He makes me feel like Cruella Deville. When he does that, I just have to put my arms around him and give him a big hug to make sure he still loves me. Of course, when I do that the training session is ended for the day. I'm not sure but I think my dog laughs at me when we walk home."

Jeanette smiles.

"As we're walking he turns around every few minutes and sticks out his tongue. I'll tell you the truth, I don't know who's in charge."

"Well, I don't know about Punch, but *I'm* laughing at you right now. What dog in his right mind is going to obey you when you hug him for doing the wrong thing? You're not supposed to do that when he *doesn't* respond to your command. When you do that you're giving him a reward for disobedience. No wonder he doesn't listen to you," said Matty.

Suppose you had a young child and he refused to do what you told him to do and you just hugged him for it. Why would he ever listen to you again? When the dog refuses to respond to a command that he's been taught, that's the time to *correct* him. You shouldn't worry about whether he will still love you because you're making demands. Dogs are better than people in some ways—they do not carry grudges. The trick is to be sure that you're correcting the dog and not punishing him. There is a big difference between the two. Punishment is when you get angry and hit him or holler at him with the crazy idea that it has something to do with dog training. Remember that you're not supposed to get angry at your dog, and punishment is doubly unfair if you haven't taught him how to perform the command in the first place. What you should do instead is correct him. A correction can be a firmly stated *No,* or a special technique for jerking the leash or both followed immediately with praise, such as "Good girl!" When you correct a puppy, you have to be extra gentle. I'll get into this subject in greater detail in Chapter Four.

"Are you telling me to treat my dog like a human?" asks Jeanette.

Matthew shakes his head and smiles.

"No, but most people who treat their dogs like kids or babies behave in a special way with them," answered Matty. "They shower them with hugs and kisses at the drop of a hat, but nobody does it when the dog refuses to obey a command. Expressing love for your dog openly in most other situations is the best thing you can do, because it makes you much more tolerant and patient with him—making him easier to train. Sometimes your dog will drive you crazy, but that's the price of enjoying life with a warm, loving friend, especially if he's a puppy. He really is like another person in your life. And even the most obstinate mischief-maker wants to please you. It's part of his doggie nature, but he just doesn't know how. It's up to you to show him what to do. You're the teacher. The dog is the student."

The Temperament Types

Before we test Punch for temperament and determine how best to train him, let's take a look at the various types of temperaments that are the most common. That way, you can refer to them as you test your own dog and figure out what you have, and what you have to do.

"So Jeanette, take the leash and hang on to Punch while I get into this."

"Okay."

She takes the leash from Matty and walks away with the dog.

There are six basic temperament or personality types, and it is quite possible for a dog to possess a combination of these traits, but that becomes obvious once you start to look at your dog in this new way. I have named the temperament categories the *Responsive; High-Energy; Strong-Willed or Stubborn; Shy; Easygoing or Sedate;* and the *Aggressive.*

The Responsive type is the easiest dog to train, although not necessarily the ideal dog for every person to live with. Responsive-type dogs really want to please you, learn quickly, and seem to enjoy the training sessions. These dogs are handled in a moderate way with a minimum of training problems. Moderate leash corrections are all that are necessary, and these dogs like generous praise as a reward for performing properly. Leash, voice, and noise corrections should be lively but not too firm. Enthusiastic praise is always a welcome reward.

The Easygoing or Sedate type is slower to move or respond to teaching and commands. These dogs hesitate before moving and never respond instantly to anything. They have to be motivated to perform properly, and this is done with firmly given commands that indicate you will not take no for an answer. Although you must be firm when commanding them, you must still be loving and affectionate. Lavish praise is essential to their training. Be patient and don't lose your temper because they do not respond to you instantly. Voice corrections are more effective than leash corrections, and it is best to use as soft a tone as possible while still being firm. A harshly given command hurts an Easygoing dog's feelings and he will look at you with pained expressions. Do not use a shake can for noise corrections with these dogs. As a matter of fact, leash corrections are rarely needed but when they are, jerk the leash in a soft-to-medium manner.

The High-Energy type is the exact opposite of the Easygoing dog. These are usually excitable, easily distracted dogs that are set off by the slightest thing that interests them, such as an exuberantly given compliment, a ringing doorbell, a person entering the room, or just about anything. High-Energy dogs by necessity must be handled firmly and with a subdued use of praise so the animal stays calm. These are fun-loving dogs who try in every way imaginable to entice you into playing with them, especially when you are trying to have a training session. They would rather play than train. These dogs require firm handling, patience, and a restrained use of praise for performing properly. Give out the praise like precious bits of gold. Corrections should be given in a precise and uncompromising manner.

The Strong-Willed type could be called plain stubborn because he wants to do things his own way or not at all. Dogs of this temperament do not generally want to be trained and challenge the entire teaching process. Your voice and body language must indicate that you will not back down, that you expect such dogs to learn what you are teaching them, and the dogs must execute the commands properly and instantly. Although you must be patient, you must also be persistent and not appear to challenge the dog. Leash corrections must be given in a medium-to-hard manner and vocal corrections must be loud and demanding.

The Shy type may be frightened by the training techniques and must be handled gently and patiently. Shy dogs are usually afraid of noises; sudden movement; strangers; or anything that is not part of their daily routine. In training, never use a leash correction or noise correction with dogs of this type. Correct them with a soft, soothing tone of voice. Lavishly praise the dog immediately following a voice correction to encourage him and rid him of his fears. Love, praise, and affection are the keys to training dogs of this kind.

The Aggressive type must be thought of in two separate categories. There are Dominant-Aggressive dogs and Fear-Aggressive dogs. Let's look at the Dominant-Aggressive type first. This type is more often a friendly dog with a powerful drive to be the top dog in all situations. They are very firm about their position in the family or pack structure. Dominant-Aggressive dogs are strong-willed and very assertive. They guard and protect their territory and usually those who live in it. These dogs can be controlling and difficult unless you can convince them that *you* are the top dog. When training these dogs you must be very aware of your body language, which should show strong-looking posture, indicating a sense of being the one in charge. This requires you to be confident and unafraid of the dog. Corrections should be given in a firm and authoritative manner. Use a light to medium leash correction accompanied by a voice correction given in a firm tone of voice. If the dog reacts aggressively to your leash corrections, discontinue use of them and seek professional help.

Fear-Aggressive dogs sometimes appear to be like Dominant-Aggressive dogs, but they are very different. The aggression in these dogs stems from insecurity and being afraid of noises; strangers; sudden movements; and anything that is not part of their daily routine. They do not see themselves as top dog nor do they want that position. Many Fear-Aggressive dogs suffer from a lack of socialization, which only compounds their problem. Fear-Aggressive dogs are often deliberately taken away from the company of people outside their families once they have demonstrated some form of aggression, and this is the worst thing that can be done. Dogs of this temperament need to be socialized with a variety of new people and places. When training them, use medium to light leash corrections along with a voice correction. The voice correction should be given in a soothing to firm tone of voice, depending on the extent of the dog's fear. Use body language that is trusting, indicating to the dog that you are nonthreatening and easy to work with. Do not tower over him in an authoritative way. Try kneeling down next to the dog as often as possible. Do not do anything that might appear intimidating to the dog, but at the same time you must maintain control over him.

Personality Evaluation

"Okay. Let's find out what Punch is really like. Pay attention to what I do, then try the same things with your own dog. This is the ideal situation for temperament testing because I've never met the dog before today. He doesn't know me and I don't know much about him. But even if your dog has been with you for a while, the tests will be valid if he has never been tested before. Punch's responses will be genuine because he doesn't know me and has no idea what I'm going to do. Remember that the point is to evaluate his personality before beginning his obedience training."

Matty takes the leash from Jeanette.

"I'm going to try out a few things with Punch and try to learn something about his temperament. Jeanette, you walk behind me and pay attention to what I do."

Matty bends over the dog, hugs him, kisses him on the nose, and then walks forward, maintaining firm control of the leash. As he walks with the dog, he guides him with the leash and continually encourages and praises him but never stops walking. Both trainer and student walk swiftly as Matty sets the quick pace, requiring Punch to keep up. They walk in a straight line for about fifteen feet, then Matty turns right and goes another fifteen feet, and then they make another right turn. Punch has no choice but to turn with him. Matty repeats the turns, making perfect squares. All the while he is walking he intermittently says the command Heel, *especially on the turns, and then instantly praises the dog in his falsetto, baby-talk voice. The enthusiasm of his voice motivates Punch to stay with him and gets the dog to walk with greater energy and interest. It also makes the session fun for the dog. Punch wags his tail excitedly and focuses his attention on Matty the whole time.*

"Come with me, buddy. Let's go. Oh, my, Mr. Punch. Look how happy you are! You are a Punch-and-Judy show all by yourself. How ya doin', buddy? Hey, Punchy!"

Matty stops suddenly, kneels down and pets the dog, and hands the leash back to Jeanette as he talks to her.

"I just accomplished two things. I established dominance over the dog by getting him to follow me and at the same time I created a bond between us. He trusts me now and accepts me as the one in charge. I even think he likes me. And, he now knows something about the command *Heel.* So, tell me some of the problems you have with him."

Jeanette frowns. "He barks when I leave him. He seems to be anxious when I go out. He's quiet when I'm around, but, boy, does he whine and bark after I leave. It tears my heart out, and it doesn't seem to do much for my neighbors, either."

"How long have you had him?"

"Two months," she replies.

"Two months? So you're practically a new dog mommy."

Jeanette smiles, "Yes."

"So here's a new owner who rescues a young dog from a shelter, who does something from the heart, but he barks when she leaves him alone. And she has to leave him during the day just like everyone else who works for a living. Leaving him behind upsets the dog, and he barks after she leaves, and he continues to bark.

"Have you tried confining him to one room, such as the kitchen, behind a puppy gate?"

"Yes, but he can jump over it. A wire dog crate is the only thing that works. Otherwise he runs around the house and jumps over things," says Jeanette.

"All right, so he jumps over everything and you put him in a crate."

She nods her head.

"So you end up confining him in a dog crate all day long, right?"

"Right."

"Okay, I get the picture. I'll tell you this, most behavior problems are resolved once the dog is obedience-trained. Now I'm not saying it's the answer to everything, but it sure solves many problems. These kinds of problems are not difficult to fix. Okay? Now, let's give the good dog a few tests to find out what he's really like."

The Roll-over Test

This test can help you select the right puppy as well as assist you in training your dog. Let me explain how it works. The first thing is to get Punch to lie on the ground with all four of his legs down. If he resists, try talking to him in a soothing way to get him to relax.

Matty places his hands on the dog's body just below the front legs and quickly turns the large dog over on his back.

"Oh, Mr. Punch. What a good boy!"

In one quick, decisive maneuver, turn him over on his

back, with his spine on the ground. Now gently hold him in place with your hand on the front of his neck. Will he stay there? Will he squirm? Will he fight you? Punch's responses, of course, determine what his temperament or personality is like. As I look at him I can see that he's insecure in this position because his back legs are coming up a little. He also has a worried look on his face. If he were totally relaxed and at ease, his legs would be straight out like a puppy lying on his back. I'm going to go a little farther with the test by putting a little pressure on him. I am going to gently grab the skin under his neck and pull it just a bit. I want to see what happens as I do this. I'm purposely going to be unresponsive to the dog's reactions for about fifteen seconds. That gives him plenty of time if he's going to react.

Look at that. For the most part he's lying calmly on the ground and seems okay with all this—but just barely. He's tense and uncertain about what's going on. If he were a completely Responsive dog, he would be a lot happier right now. He would have a cheerful expression on his face and his entire body would be relaxed.

"Jeanette, look how Punch's front paws are moving slightly in reaction to having his underside so openly exposed, and he certainly doesn't like my fingers holding the skin under his neck."

Jeanette nods her head and says, "Well, I don't think I'd care for that very much, either."

"He's not supposed to like it. But he's not supposed to mind that I did it. I can understand *his* response. I'm not so sure about you, though."

You know a lot of people identify so strongly with their dogs that they forget the difference between dogs and

In one decisive maneuver, turn the dog over on his back. Gently
hold him in place with your hand on his neck. Gently grab the skin
under his neck and pull it just a bit.

Photo by Pam Marks.

people. Never lose sight of the fact that even though dogs and people live well together, they respond differently to what happens to them and what goes on around them. This awkward thing I'm doing would not upset an even-tempered or what we call a Responsive dog. Of course a human would be uncomfortable with this no matter how easygoing he or she is.

"Repeat after me, please. I am Jeanette."

"Okay. I am Jeanette."

"I am a human."

She sighs.

"I am a human."

"Punch is a dog!"

"Okay, okay."

"Come on, say it."

"Punch is a dog. Are we through?"

"Yes, thank you, now let us not have any more identity crises, please."

Of course, if Punch had a strong-willed temperament, he would be fighting to get up and resisting any attempt on my part to hold him down. We would be having a battle royal over this. A Strong-Willed dog would give me a hard time when I tried to get him to roll over on his back. Once I got him on his back, I'm sure he would try to get my hand off his neck with his mouth and try to push me away with his paws. He would shake, rattle, and roll in a struggle to get up. He might even growl and act aggressively. A dog with a Strong-Willed temperament does not want to be held down on his back. He must be trained with firmness and with a lot of enthusiasm and encouragement.

A High-Energy dog would be moving around quite a bit to break away from the position imposed by this test. He would be mouthing my hand and complaining with all kinds of yelping and yapping. That is not the most pleasant sound. A High-Energy dog would also make it a challenge to get him on his back. The difference though is that, once you got him there, his eyes would be happy, alert, and ready for any kind of fun he can annoy you with. If you're training a High-Energy dog, you must be very calm and subdued especially when you praise him for doing the right thing. High-Energy dogs usually require firm corrections just to get them settled down.

Now a dog with an Aggressive temperament, especially a Dominant-Aggressive dog, would growl from the start. He might curl his lips and bite you if you tried to touch the skin on his neck. A Dominant-Aggressive dog will make direct eye contact with you in a threatening and challenging manner and do everything he can to avoid being on his back— and I mean everything. For him, the struggle is about being top dog. When you train a Dominant-Aggressive dog, you must be firm but friendly when giving commands. Corrections should also be exercised with firmness but with extreme caution in case the dog decides to bite. Praise, as a reward for executing the commands properly, should be given with great enthusiasm and energy.

Another kind of aggressive dog is the Fear-Aggressive dog. He will also try to bite, just like the Dominant-Aggressive dog, but he will do it out of fear and insecurity. He will try to get away from you because his aggression is defensive in nature. When you try to roll him over, he may scream, yelp, or whine loudly. He may place his body in a submissive position as he wets the floor. He will show all the signs of shyness and then bite you when you're not looking. Did you know that most dog bites, by the way, come from Fear-Aggressive dogs? These type dogs must be trained pretty much the way you would treat a Shy dog but with greater caution to avoid being bitten. When training a Fear-Aggressive dog, you must be very sensitive to his fear and insecurity, even if he is a large, protection-type dog. This means correcting him gently in most cases, with caution, and lavishing him with enthusiastic praise when he does the right thing. Fear-Aggressive dogs need a lot of confidence-building and encouragement.

A Shy dog, one with a timid, or insecure temperament, will not fight you when you try to roll him over but he will hesitate and do it slowly. His body will become very tense and constricted. In the extreme, he may scream or yelp or whine loudly. If he does, it will sound like you're killing him. A shy dog's eyes will convey fear when you try this test on him. He may try to push your hand away with his paws. His back legs will crunch upwards and his tail will tuck in over his belly, which is probably meant to protect his genitals. A Shy dog will panic and desperately try to get up.

Now let's talk about Punch. He is not exactly a Shy dog but neither is he an even-tempered or fully Responsive dog. He's somewhere in between. Let's say he's a little shy. That means you never want to be harsh with him during training. You must not yell at him or raise your voice. Punch is going to need a more sensitive touch when you train him, which means his corrections must be softer and gentler than ordinarily given.

"Oh, yes. You're a good boy, my Punchy. Oh, Matty's proud."

Let's move on to the next test.

The Social Attraction Test

The next most important temperament test is the Social Attraction Test. I make a whimpering sound like a puppy or a dog that wants something. I will whimper and then talk to the dog affectionately until I get a reaction. His reaction will tell us how friendly he is and whether he responds in a socially acceptable way. It also shows us whether he is a curious dog. The reaction I anticipate is for Punch to look at me, get excited, and be happy. But, you know every dog is different, just like people. Okay. Let's see if he's alert. If he looks at me, jumps at me in a friendly way, or comes over to me to play, to get some attention, or just to satisfy his curiosity, I will know that he's friendly, alert, and responsive in social situations and with strangers. This is very important for his training. Now, let's see what he does. I'm going to be about six feet away. I'll kneel down because I don't want to present any threatening body language.

Matty begins to whimper like a dog and then talks to Punch in his high-pitched tone.

"Oh Punch, you're my boy. Come here, honey. Come here, Punch."

He continues to whimper like a puppy that wants attention.

"Look, he's coming over to me. This is great."

Punch didn't jump on me and he's just a little hesitant. With this information about him I know I will get the best training results if I am gentle with him throughout the course. As a matter of fact, that is the only way to handle him for the rest of his life and in all situations. If he came over to me and jumped all over me, then I would say he was a real outgoing guy and could be handled in a much firmer manner, which makes the training go faster when you're teaching obedience commands.

"What do you think, Jeanette? Would you say he's a little Shy?"

"Yes. I have to admit that it never occurred to me that he was like that. This changes everything, doesn't it?"

"That right."

If Punch had been distracted, jumped all over the place, or been out of control but not menacing, I would have said he was a Strong-Willed dog requiring a firm hand. If he had whined, backed away, barked, looked curious but reticent, crawled to me, held his tail down and his ears back, licked my hand seeking reassurance, then I would have said he was a Shy, very timid, or insecure dog requiring kid-glove treatment when being trained. If he had looked at me without moving or was only mildly interested and then lost interest completely, or came over to me slowly, or turned away, I would have concluded that he was an Easygoing or Sedate dog requiring a firm hand for training. On the other hand, if Punch had lunged, curled his lips, growled, or acted too bold with his ears erect and his tail held straight up I would have said he was a Dominant-Aggressive dog. In that case, I would have to be very firm when handling him, and I might even place a soft nylon muzzle on him to avoid being bitten.

The Hand-Shy Test

The next test is the Hand-Shy Test. Its purpose is to determine if your dog has ever been punished by being hit with something like a rolled-up newspaper or slapped with a bare hand. It is important to know about this because your dog must trust you if you are going to teach him obedience commands. If your dog has been hit in the past, you may make an innocent gesture that is misinterpreted by him as threatening because it seems like you're going to hit him. Obedience training a dog requires using your hands for many things such as teaching hand signals and touching his body at specific times in specific ways. It is important to know ahead of time whether your dog is hand-shy or not.

The test is simple. All you do is take your hand and pretend to hit your dog. Obviously I don't want you to actually hit him. Please, don't even scare him. Uncle Matty would *not* be so proud. It's a test and we're looking for information. If he's two or three years old or more, and you feel certain he might bite you, then you should definitely skip this test. But if he's a young dog that you think is safe to handle, raise your hand above your head in a threatening manner.

The large dog flinches and shrinks away from Matty.

"See how he reacts to my hand? That was the hand part of the test. Let's try the voice part of the test.

"Now I'll just raise my voice and say, 'Punch! No, no, no!'"

Punch slinks away with a hurt look on his face.

"It's okay, Punchy. You're a good boy. You are. It's okay. I love you. I'm sorry. I didn't mean to scare you."

He turns to Jeanette.

"You can see how frightened he is of my raised hand and of my disapproving, punishing tone of voice, which means someone hit him at some point in his life and yelled at him, too. He may even have been abused on a continual basis. This is important information about your dog. This alters the way you must relate to this dog. Jeanette, your assignment is to convince Punch that you love him, that he is safe with you, that he can trust you not to be abusive in any way. If you accomplish that, you will have a well-trained, very happy, loving pet."

He turns to the dog with understanding, sympathy, and an apologetic tone of voice.

"Okay, Punch. It's okay. I'm sorry, I didn't mean it. I really didn't."

Punch is a fairly large dog. If he was an Aggressive dog and I did that, there is a good chance he might have bitten me. You have to be careful because you can't be sure of your dog's reaction to this test.

"Let's make sure everyone understands that I never hit him, right?"

Jeanette agrees.

"All right. Have *you* ever hit the dog?"

"No," she answers.

"But somebody did something, which is why he flinched when I tested him. Don't forget he had a previous owner, and you don't know what happened before you adopted him from the shelter. Now we tested him with my hand. Let's see what happens when I try it with a rolled-up newspaper."

Matty picks up a rolled-up newspaper and holds it above his head. Punch cowers and is obviously frightened by the gesture. The dog gives a low, throaty growl.

"Listen to that. That's a dog that has had troubles with newspapers."

Matty apologizes to the dog in a soothing, gentle tone of voice.

"Okay. I'm sorry. Uncle Matty knows. I'll never do it again, I promise."

Now, what we've learned is that Punch is afraid of being hit with a bare hand or with a newspaper and of being yelled at. If you or anyone else threatens him, he will not only bark but he may become aggressive. Once your dog feels secure in his new home and knows you're coming back every day, and once he is obedience-trained, he may very well stop barking simply because you left him home.

Punch needs to be reconditioned so he's no longer afraid of anyone's hand. This can be accomplished by taking my hand and rubbing his back as I talk to him in a sweet, loving way. I will start from the back because I don't want to scare him. Then I would talk to him as I rub and say things like, Good boy, what a guy. I will just keep rubbing his back gently and tenderly, moving my hands up slowly toward his head, talking lovingly to him. What a good boy. Always use your voice as gently as you use your hand. What a good boy. Then I will give him a treat, some kind of tidbit that I know he likes. All right? I will bring it to him and let him see it before I give it to him, like this. Hold it above his head. Keep talking as you attempt to give him the treat but from a little farther away. Good boy. The idea is for him to begin to relate to your raised hand in an entirely different way. Your hands should only be used for pleasant things, such as back rubs, and giving food treats, and expressions of affection. Oh, Matty's proud. Again, lavish him with more love and more affection. Then I should be able to go like this . . . watch.

He raises his hand with the treat in it, but the dog does not flinch this time. His fear of the raised hand seems to be gone.

"Good boy! Oh, I'm so proud! See, he's less frightened of my hand now. Oh, Matty's proud. Punch, you got an *A*.

I'm so proud. Of course, this requires a great deal of repetition to make him less fearful of the human hand."

The Pain-Tolerance Test

This is another test that I'd like to give Punch. I call it the Pain-Tolerance Test. Its purpose is to find out if your dog is overly sensitive to being pulled or grabbed by the skin. In other words, how much tolerance does he have for discomfort and minor pain? Suppose you have children in the house, or you bring home a new baby, or you want to comb and brush the dog for the first time. You need to know how much touching, grabbing, pulling, and exuberant play your dog will tolerate and whether or not he will get nasty. This test is good for childproofing your dog. It is also important so you can determine how much correction your dog is able to tolerate. It's very important for training.

In this test you touch certain parts of the dog's body in a firm, annoying manner. Most dogs do not respond negatively. However, pain-sensitive areas could cause a lack of tolerance because of painful medical conditions, such as hip dysplasia, skin sores, or any number of ailments. If a dog has been hit or abused in the past, he will certainly be sensitive to being grabbed or pulled by the skin. A lack of tolerance for pain or discomfort could be inherited because of poor breeding, or could be the result of abusive behavior from humans in his past life. Every dog has a different level of tolerance to physical discomfort. The results of this test will establish your puppy's level of tolerance. It will tell you how sensitive you have to be when you're handling the dog in everyday activities and particularly in training so no one gets bitten. It is important to know how much roughhousing from a child your dog will accept and how to correct the dog when you are training him.

What we want to do is check out the various areas of his body. If you are testing a dog that is more than ten months old, you must be cautious because you could be seriously injured if he decides to bite you. Go to a nice quiet place for this test, where there are no spectators. The last thing you need is an audience. When you begin the test start very gently and then slowly increase the level of discomfort. Use your fingers and your hands to do the test and control the dog with a leash and collar.

There are three places on Punch's body that should be tested: the tail, the toes, and the rump. Let's do the rump first.

"Jeanette, I think you better take a step or two back so he doesn't snap indiscriminately. The first thing I'll do is pull the skin on his back just a bit. Notice I am pulling gently at first but now I'm pulling harder. I'm increasing the pressure.

"Are you okay with this?"

Jeanette looks nervous and says, "You're not hurting my dog, are you? I'd hate that a lot."

Matty shakes his head and stops what he's doing. He puts his arm around her and whispers.

"Please trust me. This is Uncle Matty. Look at my face. Is this the face of someone who would hurt a dog? Are we clear?"

Jeanette nods. Matthew repeats his statement.

"Are we clear?"

"Yes, but let's just do it. I don't like it. I have to tell you

Gently pull back the skin on his back, just a bit. With your finger and thumb, press lightly between his toes, expanding them out-

ward. Giving this test depends on the age of the dog and your common sense. Photos by Pam Marks.

the truth, the name of this test puts me off. You call it the Pain-Tolerance Test. What does that mean?"

"It means you haven't seen what I'm about to do. Once you do, I want to hear you say 'Gee, Uncle Matty, I'm sorry for making such a fuss.' If it makes you feel any better, I'll call it the Sensitivity Test, okay?"

Jeanette nods but is near tears. Matthew continues.

We have so far learned that Punch has good tolerance. He's not growling at me. If he were growling at me, obviously he would be in pain. It didn't bother him at all. That's good. That's really good. At least you know that if a kid grabbed him like that, he's not going to growl. When doing this test, the dog is safe if he looks at you as if it were a game. If he tries to snap at you, then he has average tolerance; but if he screams and tries to bite, he has poor pain tolerance and is not recommended to be around very young, rambunctious children. If he growls and then tries to bite, or if he bites without warning, he must not be with any children, even well-intended kids who might unintentionally grab him.

"Now let's test him on the tail. Jeanette, you hold the dog in place with the leash. I'm going to grab his tail and pull it gently. Look, he is not upset at all. It just doesn't bother him. This is excellent."

The dog is absolutely safe if he just turns around and mouths your hand and does not seem bothered. If he is comfortable with what you are doing but tries to stop you, moves away, or mouths your hand, or if he starts to cry or whimper but does not show signs of aggression, then he has a good pain tolerance and little or no physical sensitivity. On the other hand, if the dog howls and screams when you pull his tail, growls, curls his lips, snaps, or tries to get away, then his tolerance is poor and he will not make a great playmate for young kids. If he bites and growls when you pull his tail, then he should not even be around kids.

"The last part of the test involves his toes. Please hold him in place, Jeanette, while I test him. First, let's put him in a *Sit* position. *Sit!* Good boy. Good Punch."

Okay, now I take one of his paws in my hand and, with my finger and thumb, I press lightly between his toes, expanding them outward. I am gradually increasing the pressure for a few seconds until he starts to show some sign of discomfort. Good boy. He's pretty good with this too, so he's just fine.

"Good boy."

Performing this test depends on the age of the dog and your common sense. You don't want to take a three-year-old dog that's growled at people and start grabbing him if you already know it makes him dangerous. You already know what you need to know without the tests.

"Okay, Jeanette, have you got all this?"

"Oh, sure, Matty. I'm now the world's leading authority based on what you just taught me."

Uncle Matty grabs the leash and starts to run up the beach with Punch. He yells back at her as he heads toward the ocean.

"Just read the chapter a couple of times until you have it all down pat."

Two
The Bonds of Friendship

My word is my bond. Actually, my *dog* is my bond. If you like, you can refer to me as a bond salesman. I can play these word games all day because the subject is as important as it is enjoyable. To bond with your dog is to create a relationship with him based on the friendship, love, caring, and trust that make living with a dog so incredible. As far as I know, bonding with your dog was an unknown idea when I first began training dogs more than thirty years ago. Although bonding with a dog was *not* my idea, I have bonded with every dog I have ever trained since I first learned about the concept. I believe that bonding with your dog is the most important thing you can do, especially as a preparation for obedience training. If you bond with your dog, you will have the best relationship possible and training will be as much fun as it will be successful. A dog is going to be your responsibility, like a child, for the next fifteen or so years, and what you do now is going to decide what kind of dog you're going to have for the rest of your lives together. Everything you do to create the bond is crucial.

I'm always asked what is the most important part of owning a dog. And those who ask always add to the question, "It's dog training, isn't it?" I always answer by saying that training is not the most important thing. Bonding is more important.

"Bonding?" asked Gretchen Stebbins. "What's that? Sounds like some Wall Street thing."

Matty shakes his head.

"Do you mind waiting until I introduce you?"

"No, but my husband and my dog are going to burst soon if you don't hurry up."

"Okay, okay. I'll be right with you. Let me make some points here. Hey, whose book is it anyway? Where was I? Oh, yes. Bonding, I say, is at the heart of owning your dog. You know what, Gretchen, I'll bring you into it now. Let me ask you what it is that you want me to do for you?"

The woman, holding her young dog on a taut leash, answers eagerly.

"I want you to train my dog, and I would appreciate it if it could happen sometime before we qualify for AARP membership. I want Frank to be obedient. And, gee, I'd like you to get him to stop pulling me down the street like a sled."

"And would Frank be the dog?"

Matty takes the leash from her and walks briskly away as the dog runs after him.

She calls to him, "Of course he's the dog. His name is Frank. You're very funny."

Using his falsetto tone of voice, Matty gets the dog all excited.

"Come on, let's go. Oh, what a good boy! Oh, Mister Frank. Matty's proud."

Matty returns and comes to a full stop after a number of quick turns and sudden stops. He tightens the leash above the dog's head with his left hand and pushes his rear end down with his right. He looks at the young dog and gives him a firm command. Sit. *The dog sits on his haunches in an obedient manner. Matty then puts his hand in front of the dog's eyes and speaks softly but with authority. He carefully tells the dog* Stay *each time he starts to leave the Sit position. Matty continues to hold the leash above the dog's head and in a subdued tone of voice talks to him as he remains in the position.*

"Thank you. *Stay.*"

He tightens on the leash as the dog tries to go to him.

"*Stay!* Thank you. Thank you very much."

Like a lion tamer, he quietly drops the leash from his hand and slowly walks away from the dog, who does not move from his sitting position. The owner stands quietly impressed. She can hardly speak. All that's missing is the applause.

"Now, if I may continue. Thank you. And you *Stay,* too."

Dog training comes second because bonding comes first. Look what I was able to do with this dog by establishing instant rapport with him before putting him in a Sit position. That quick running conversation I had with him was just a bit of bonding along with a few other things. Most people I meet really want a dog they can love, who will love them back. They want a friend, someone to take walks with. And if they're really honest about it, they want someone to talk to, someone who will really listen. A dog will do all that plus snuggle with you. What more could you want? No matter what you want from your dog, it has to start with the creation of a bond between you.

"You call that a bond? So let me get this straight. One run down the street and you're bonded?" said Gretchen sarcastically.

Matty smiles.

"Not exactly, but look how nicely he's sitting. It was a quick, temporary thing and a good start of the process. What does it take to impress you? I just wanted him to stop interrupting me so I could finish my sentence. I haven't completely bonded with him and he hasn't been completely trained. That's all ahead. Trust me. Besides, it's more important that you and your husband bond with Frank."

Think about it. What do mothers and fathers do with young children? They hold them; they take care of them; they love them; and they nurture them. That's what has to be done for all children, from conception to commencement and after that, too. This is especially important when they're very young. Well, guess what? That's bonding. The same is true for dogs, no matter how old they are.

"Let's talk about you and your dog for a minute."

"Okay, let's talk about him."

"Do you mind? I'm talking to them. You're not the only one here, you know.

"Nurturing establishes the bond between the dog and all members of the family. Once the bond exists, which simply means that once the love, affection, and dedication are there, then the training can begin. If you don't bond first, you may have a well-trained dog with no personality and with no emotional ties to you. So what's the point of having him? Okay, get ready. I'm going to repeat what I said before. This is really important. Bonding means creating a close, personal relationship with your dog by expressing love, praise, and affection. Once that's established, you build on it and accomplish anything you want, including obedience training. One more thing: Everyone in your home should be involved with creating that bond."

"Well, there's just me and my husband, Wally," said the mischievous dog owner.

"That's more than enough. Look, your dog is a member of the family now and should be treated like one. Establishing a bond does exactly that. Remember, first you bond, then you train."

"Okay, okay. You're getting on my nerves. You must have said the word bonding a hundred times already."

Matty shakes his head and sighs.

"Why do I do it? Why do I put up with this?"

"It must be the money," says Gretchen.

"You're right, it's the money. I keep repeating the word bonding so none of you forget it. It's the most important part of owning a dog."

"Please, Matthew, sweetheart, I beg you. Don't say that word again, okay? It's getting on my nerves."

"Okay. I'll stop saying it. Now let's talk about you."

I am standing inside a very beautiful home nestled in the lush Philadelphia Main Line, and I'm with Gretchen and Wallace Stebbins. The couple are the proud owners of Frank, a six-month-old German Shepherd Dog.

"Frank? What kind of a name is that for a German shepherd? Sounds more like a barber than a dog. Hey, you can't write this stuff. Well, actually, you can. Hi, Gretchen."

"Finally. Hello, Matthew. This is my husband, Wally."

"Hi, Wally. So, what's with Frank?"

Gretchen steps forward as she hangs on to the young, rambunctious dog that is no longer in the Sit position and is pulling on the leash as hard as he can to get to Matty for a good face licking. Matty smiles at the dog and cups his face in his hands.

"Okay, Frankie, I'm gonna get back to you in a minute. Settle down. *Sit!*"

The dog licks his lips and goes into a perfect Sit position.

"Stay!"

The dog does not move.

"That was quick," says Gretchen. "How'd you do that?"

"You know how I did it. Frank and I, well you know, the *B* word."

"Don't say it."

"I won't say . . ." *he whispers*, ". . . bonding."

She giggles and continues, "We love the dog, but he never listens to us. He pulls too hard on the leash, and walking him is a humiliating experience. He's got more energy and strength than I do and I can barely keep up with him. My neighbors laugh at me when Frank drags me down the street. He needs to be trained."

Her husband interrupts, "You know, Uncle Matty—may I call you Uncle Matty?"

"Sure."

"Well, Uncle Matty, I'm not a cream puff but this dog really gets to me, and I just don't have the heart to yank him down the street or holler at him even though he is unmanageable."

Gretchen laughs.

She pokes him in the ribs with her elbow and says, "And that's a riot because when we first got the dog Wally didn't want him and hardly looked at him."

Matty turns to the man who is wearing maroon golf pants, a lime-green shirt, spiked shoes, and is toying with a number-two wood.

"How could you not want this dog? He's wonderful!"

"I know that now, but I didn't know that then. *Now* I want him, *then* I didn't," says Wally. "I was upset when we first got him."

"Why?"

Wally, embarrassed, looks down at his shoes and mumbles.

"I can't hear you. Wally, please speak up."

Wally raises his voice.

"Well, I didn't like the breed. I thought they were all just a bunch of police dogs. I thought they were dangerous animals that bite people and I didn't think I wanted to live with that. I just wanted a big orange dog, you know, something from a Disney movie."

Matty looks amused and answers gently.

"Oh, you wanted Old Yeller! Or was it Big Red? Don't you know that German Shepherds are great dogs? Any dog of any breed, and I mean any breed, could be either Old Yeller or a dangerous biter depending on the behavior he inherits and the way he was treated before you got him. So what changed your mind about Frankie?"

Wally looks sheepish and says, "Well, I guess it was his playful face, with one ear up and one ear down and, ah, what can I say, I fell for him."

Matty chuckles.

"What? You went soft for Frank, that vicious beast?"

On hearing his name the playful dog breaks from his Sit position, jumps on Matty, and licks his face. Matty sits on the ground and grabs Frank's young body and wrestles with him.

"Okay, okay. You win, Mr. Frank."

"Of course, you must realize that this is a German Shepherd Dog and as a breed they are territorial. Which also means they are naturally protective. Frank here is obviously not an Aggressive dog, as far as I'm concerned, although I'm sure he will become protective as he matures. But it's clear to me that he has a dominant personality, no doubt about it. In other words, if you're not strong with him, he'll be strong with you. So you have to be the top dog, the leader of his pack, okay?"

Gretchen and Wally nod.

"Frankie is a wonderful puppy, a really nice dog, and you're going to have a fabulous time with him. The thing is if you're a soft person, too easygoing, if you want to baby him, he's not the right dog for you. Eventually you're going to have to be strong owners in order to control him. He's a good dog, though, and as you already know, it won't be hard to love him and appreciate him more and more as time goes by. He is going to teach you a lot. Not only that, he is probably going to change the way you behave.

"What's going to help enormously here . . ."

Wally and Gretchen chime together, "We know, bonding."

"You know, dogs are much nicer than people. If there were more dogs than people, heartburn would be stamped out forever. Give me a room full of dogs any day. Please, allow me to tell you what you have to do. This is important. Pay attention."

Almost immediately after a mother gives birth to a new baby she is handed the infant to hold, hug, and adore. If the dad is smart enough to be in the delivery room at the time, he is also encouraged to hold the newborn baby and love it as soon as possible. An instant emotional bond is created between the parents and the baby when they look at each other for the first time. Something magical happens that can last a lifetime. There is instant contact, instant love. Now let's take the same idea and apply it to bringing a dog home for the first time, especially a puppy. Who can resist placing its sweet face next to your own and giving it a big hug and a kiss? The warmth of your cheek next to the warmth of the dog is powerful stuff. When you do that, you start the bonding process, and it can only get better from there.

"Gretchen, let me ask you this. Has there ever been anything more exciting than the day you brought your new dog home?"

As she thinks about it she gets teary-eyed and smiles.

"No. We don't have children so I'm not sure what that's like but I suspect it's similar. I remember when we brought Frank home. It was last March. I was into it; my husband wasn't."

Matty pursues Wally.

"Okay, Wally, so what did you do? Or should I ask, what didn't you do?"

"Well, Uncle Matty, I'm embarrassed to say it, but I used to leave the room whenever my wife brought in the dog. I was mad at her for getting him without telling me about it. She would carry him into the living room and I would go upstairs to my office and check out a few legal briefs, you know, just to avoid seeing the dog."

"What changed?"

"Well, it was Frank who did it. Somehow he got away from Gretchen, ran up the stairs like a demon, and scurried into my office like he was being chased. He was a dog on a mission. The door was wide open and it never occurred to me that he would just barge in. This little guy was determined to get under my skin and make me love him. Well, what are you going to do when a big clumsy puppy, with one ear up and another one down, jumps into your lap and won't stop sticking his cold nose in your ear? I lost that game. It was a shut out. No hits, no runs, no errors and I had the home-team advantage, too. The dog caught me off guard. Ever since then I found myself playing Jack Benny to his George Burns. He just wrapped me around his paw and now I can't help myself. I'm hooked. I can't remember what it was like without him."

"That's a nice story. Of course that is what I would call . . ."

Wally and Gretchen shake their heads and say in unison, "Don't mention the word."

"I won't. I won't. I was going to say building. Binding? How about bending? Imagine trying to ignore a dog like this? It can't be done. But you know there's still more you-know-what to be done. Accepting the dog and even becoming devoted to him is not going to get him trained or get him to walk properly on leash. There is still more of the, ah, *B* word to be done. You have to develop a full relationship with Frank, so it's firmly established in his mind that you are the leaders of his pack. If you want a great dog, then you have to accept the fact that there's a lot to be done and it's more important than anything else, even golf. And that goes for you, too, Gretchen."

"What did I do?" she replies defensively.

"It's about what hasn't been done. Let me tell you how the process works. In order to you-know-what, you simply do all the normal everyday things you always do but you do them with the dog.

"Let him follow you around as you do your chores in and out of the house. Hug him; talk to him; touch him as you feed him; brush him; walk him; and do all the other essential things you do for him. But there's even more to it. In addition to all that, you have to allow the dog to be a youngster who makes mistakes. Do not expect perfection at this young age. Have faith that all his misbehaving is going to get straightened out and then go about the business of completing the process before you train him. It won't take long, I promise. Forget punishments, forget hollering at him, and forget scolding him. These are harmful, especially when you're in the process of . . ." *he whispers* ". . . you-know-what.

"Oh, and another thing. If you had a Shy dog and carried him around in your arms all day thinking you were bonding with him, you would be making a big mistake. Doing that is not good for a dog because, in that situation, he will connect only to the person holding him rather than becoming social with everyone he comes in contact with. It also tends to make the dog helpless."

Gretchen protests, "I don't do that. Look at the size of this dog."

"Of course you don't. But some dog owners do. I wasn't referring to you. It was a general statement. I'm not just talking to you, you know. I've never used a leash correction on a human before but you're tempting me. May I please continue?

"If you want to create a friendly dog, a dog that's a real pleasure to live with, who gets along with most people, then do the things I'm about to suggest. You must get the dog to interact with as many different people and dogs as possible so you create a social animal that is comfortable in most situations. One of the most important reasons for doing this is to create a friendly dog that establishes relationships with lots of people, not just you and your immediate family.

"Now Frank is a friendly dog because fortunately he was born that way. But I doubt if he's been formally socialized."

Gretchen becomes defensive and says, "What are you talking about? Of course he's been socialized. What does it mean, socialized? It's not some political thing is it?"

Matty points his finger at her.

"Gottcha. Okay, let me explain a few things about socialization."

Important research exists that demonstrates that a dog's personality and adaptability to humans can be extremely influenced from the third to the seventh week of his life. Of course the dog's personality continues to be shaped after that, but this period is critical. Puppies that have been gently and lovingly handled at least once or twice a day by humans from the twenty-first to the forty-ninth day of their lives have been *socialized*. This means they will get along well with humans and have no trouble accepting them as pack leaders. It also means they will be easier to train. Most good breeders and animal professionals believe this is true and make it their business to socialize their new litters of puppies. But wait, there's more.

You have to go a step or two further and *make* your dog social. It is possible that a foolish dog owner can undo all the good effects of socialization with poor handling and by making serious mistakes with a puppy or young dog. By creating strong emotional ties with your dog, and then exposing him to as many people, noises, places, and situations that you can, you reinforce the early socialization technique.

Encourage your dog to become social with other people and dogs by taking him everywhere you go in your car, on shopping trips, to visit with your friends, and wherever else he's allowed to enter. This has a great influence on the process. Allow friendly people to pet him as long as they don't get him too excited or upset him in any way. Being petted by others will make him social outside his family and get him accustomed to new people and places.

"I think this is very important, especially for a dominant dog like Frank who, under certain circumstances, can become an Aggressive dog. I don't think you'll get an argument from Frank about being taken everywhere. Most dogs like that."

"Are there specific things we can do to successfully, you know, accomplish that thing you keep saying with the dog?" asks Gretchen.

"Of course. There are lots of specifics but I have to warn you, there is no way to discuss them without saying . . . that word."

Wally pats Matthew on the back and reassures him. "It's okay, use the *B* word all you want, Uncle Matty. We don't mind anymore. Right, Gretchen?"

She nods.

Okay, then. Because new puppies have no inhibitions, training, or physical control, they are going to soil the floor whenever they need to and wherever they happen to be. That means you must begin some form of housebreaking or paper training immediately. But I urge you to be as gentle as possible and avoid harsh discipline when doing this. Your puppy needs to get comfortable in his new home, and strict training from the first day interferes with the creation of a bond between you. Let him sniff around, learn where everything is, and get to know you before getting down to business.

It is wrong to think that you must never spoil your puppy. Puppies should be controlled, but it's a mistake to badger them with any kind of harsh discipline for every little thing they do that isn't right. Puppies have to make mistakes while they're young, it's their birthright. Be patient and understanding. You have to be a parent as well as a teacher. The idea is to nurture your little dog with the goal of creating the bond. It is far more important at the start of your life with this dog for you and everyone else to get to know him and treat him with tender, loving care, with hugging, touching, and talking. You'll get much more that way than with inappropriate discipline.

One important point I'd like to make has to do with naming your dog. Give him a friendly name and then use it frequently. This is not only good for the dog but keeps you in a pleasant frame of mind when you deal with him. If you name your dog Stupid or Barf Bag, it will be reflected in your manner. There is simply no way to call a dog Stupid in a nice way.

Talking It Up

Bonding depends on your willingness to talk to your dog. Most people talk to their dogs, especially if they think no one is listening. There is nothing so satisfying as a nice long talk with a good friend. And what better listener can there be than your best friend? He doesn't interrupt. He doesn't offer unwanted advice. And he never, never, never judges you. When you talk to him remember that it's not the words you say but rather the sound of your voice and the feeling that lies underneath it that communicate your feelings. Your dog will know exactly how you feel about him and yourself by the way you use your voice. Think about it.

How would you talk to a new baby? Everybody sounds ridiculous when they do it. Have you ever held a baby in front of you and peered deeply into his or her eyes and said the most meaningful things, just before you plunge into the goo-goo, ga-ga, boopy-doopy stuff? But babies love it, because underneath the words and sounds, approval, playfulness, and love are being communicated. Even though you're making a fool out of yourself, you know the baby adores it. It must be true because they smile, squeal in delight, or listen very seriously with their eyes open as wide as saucers. New babies are utterly captivated by everyone and everything, so long as you pay attention to and talk to them. It's impossible to measure the influence this kind of attention has, but you have to know it's great.

The human voice affects puppies pretty much the same way. They, too, will concentrate on you when you talk to them. Always be gentle with your little dog and avoid loud, angry tones. The higher you set your voice, the happier the puppy will be, and as an added bonus he will also become curious, energized, and responsive. My Uncle Matty high-pitched falsetto sound said with enthusiasm really gets a puppy going. There is no doubt that a soothing or playful sounding voice helps create the emotional bond between you and your dog. Your hands and your voice are two of the most important tools for the bonding process.

These are the tools for shaping a relationship with your dog that will last for the rest of his life.

Try using my Uncle Matty tone of voice even if you think it sounds silly. You cannot imagine how effectively it establishes a dog's trust, interest, and enthusiasm. It works miracles. That sound creates a happy frame of mind in any dog and makes all of them willing to do anything in the world for you. Of course it looks silly to the rest of the world. Just imagine getting on your knees in front of a puppy and squeaking out in a falsetto voice, "Oh my, Dr. Dog. How are you today? Let's go to work and train some people. Are you ready for that? My, my, my, my, my! Good dog!"

You get the idea. It's crazy, but most people will understand if they see you do this with your dog. If you want to feel really silly, try singing to your dog. There's nothing wrong with trying to entertain your dog. You'd do it for any loved one, wouldn't you? What's wrong with curling up with a nice, warm puppy in your arms and singing it to sleep? Not only will you help the bonding process, you just may get yourself a nice night's sleep in the bargain. Let's hear those voices sing along. The sound of a wolf howling in the night is a version of canine singing and is an unforgettable thing. If it's good enough for wolves, it is certainly good enough for a puppy.

Hold Me, Touch Me

Once you see it, you have to touch it.

"I don't think I like this," says Gretchen.

"Well, this isn't what you think it is. These are the specifics of bonding that you asked for. I'm talking about petting and stroking your puppy's belly. It's about bonding. But why do I have to explain this to you?"

"Okay, but I'm listening carefully, so watch it."

"Thank you. Who can resist a plump little belly and those sweet eyes."

"I'm still listening."

"And I'm still talking about bonding. Go on, touch it. You'll be glad you did. It needs to be rubbed."

"That's it! I'm leaving."

"Good."

Your puppy's plump little stomach is one of the best places to pet him. It can actually put him to sleep. Rub it, pet it, scratch it, and gently push it in with your hand. It's not only natural, it's good for you and the dog. You cannot bond effectively with your dog unless you touch him affectionately, and puppies make this easy to do because they crave physical contact. In the first few days of his life, before all his bodily systems begin to function on their own, your dog's mother licks him on the belly to get his digestive processes working. It is a biological gesture that helps newborns survive. So when you rub your dog's belly, you evoke for your dog a sensual memory of the first few days of his life, reminding him of the warmth, comfort, and safety provided by his mother.

If you have ever watched a litter of puppies in the first week or two of their lives, you have seen how they pile on top of one another and draw from each other's warmth. The mother dog picks them up in her mouth and moves them around from place to place. She licks them clean. She nuzzles them with her nose. She gently shoves them with her paws and gets them moving. At feeding time, the puppies pile together, competing to get a fair share of milk. When they nap, they stack on top of one another and look like a heap of dog. They are sensual creatures and live mostly by sight, sound, touch, and smell. There is little thought about these things. Physical contact and warmth is what puppies need. If you love your dog, it is important to express this with your hands and your voice. New dog owners just can't get over it when their young dogs ask to be petted by placing their head on or near their owner's hands. The gesture is very touching. Physical contact is very important to the bonding process. Do not be inhibited about this. Play with your dog, rub him, pet him, and by all means express your affection with your hands. If you can do that, you can bond with your dog in a very short period of time.

The House He Lives In

Creating the bond also involves teaching your puppy about his new home. You must allow the dog to explore his new territory, with your supervision of course. Your dog will quickly learn where he eats, where he sleeps, and where he is allowed to play and wander. It is a good idea to lead the new dog into each room of your home so he can see it, smell it, and understand what it has to do with him. By doing this you help him define his boundaries and understand when he oversteps them. Introduce him to the place where he is supposed to sleep, and see to it that he always uses it by providing him with a comfortable bed or blanket and always returning his toys there. Place his food and water bowl in the same place, usually the kitchen, and always feed him there. Be very positive and upbeat in the way you handle these things. Whenever you bring the dog to a new area that is his, reward him for being there and give him lots of praise. Never allow him to develop negative associations with the various areas that pertain to him. Dogs require their own territory but will be satisfied with a portion of your territory because they consider themselves part of the pack that you lead.

Playing Around

Old dogs as well as puppies like to play because it involves learning basic survival skills and practicing them. When you toss a ball to your dog you are re-creating his instinct to give chase. Although play is fun for your dog, it is also something he needs to do to satisfy his nature. When you satisfy your dog's essential needs, such as food, shelter, affection, and play, you cannot help but bond with him. Play with your dog whenever you have some free time, assuming he wants it. Play can involve exercise, tossed toys, hide-and-seek, long walks and runs, all ending with happy talk, lots of praise, and an occasional food treat.

When you play with your dog do not get rough. The bonding process stops if you engage in games that encourage aggressive behavior. Tug-of-war; boxing; tripping; sock pulling; and pretend growling are negative and work against the bonding process. Play might involve getting down to the dog's level and clowning around verbally, making faces, rolling around and manipulating his toys, but not in a teasing manner. Your play should include cuddling, hugging, and even massaging. Never, never allow your dog to nip or bite your fingers, no matter how gently he does it. It not only works against bonding, it helps to create an aggressive dog that will not be cute as he gets older. Remember, if the dog misbehaves, do *not* hit him. The rule of thumb is to do only those things with your dog that you would do with a baby.

In a Family Way

Bonding is for everyone in your home. It is important that the entire family and anyone else living with you try to establish a relationship with the dog. Naturally, not everyone can relate to the dog in the same way. Some family members are more outgoing than others but may not be good at expressing their feelings. For others, the reverse may be true. Everyone is different. Everything will be fine as long as everyone living in the house accepts the new dog as a member of the family. If they do, they will find their own way to develop a relationship with him.

In every home there is usually one person who winds up doing everything for the dog. Often it is the mother in the house. The truth is, it would be best if everyone shared the responsibilities for the dog's needs. For example, the first person out of bed and dressed should be the one to give the puppy his first walk of the day, and that can vary from day to day. Someone else can give him his meal. When all of the dog's needs are shared, the bond will develop quickly with everyone.

From the day the dog arrives, everyone in the house should make as great a fuss over him as possible. But it becomes hard to find takers for the dog's care once the newness wears off. Some members of the family will continue to be enthusiastic about the dog, others may not. That is to be expected. However, everyone must make an effort to bond with the dog no matter what. A person doesn't have to go gaga every time they see the dog. Just talk to him, touch him, and do one small thing for him each day. That goes far in establishing a lasting tie with the animal.

Children are often competitive for their parents' attention and may see the new dog as a rival. This is nothing to be too concerned about unless the insecure child harms the dog or acts out his or her anger. More often than not a new puppy in the house is such an exciting event that there is no room or time for jealousy or rivalry. A new dog is a good thing most of the time. A child may regard his or her pet as a new friend. Parents may see the new puppy as just another child to look after. How it all sorts out does not matter as long as the dog is treated well and bonds with everyone.

Bonding Things to Do

Whatever you do for your dog, do it while you are expressing your good feelings about him. Make simple things like feeding seem special by making a fuss over the activity. Add excitement and enthusiasm to a walk. Since many dogs have a hard time accepting baths, be exceptionally soothing and comforting just before and right after you bathe him. Immediately after a bath comb and brush out his coat. This is a great opportunity to hug the dog and stroke his body affectionately while actually getting something practical accomplished. Brush him gently. If you use a coat conditioner, the comb and or brush will not snag and hurt him. This is important so the dog does not associate this activity with pain.

Take your dog with you wherever you go. Get him to follow you around as you straighten up the house, fix things, and even talk on the phone. Anything that involves movement can be play for a dog, and play is a form of exercise. Exercise is good for bonding no matter how it comes about. Bonding occurs when you play with your dog. Play is an important bonding activity. Games, exercise, and all other kinds of play excite and invigorate all dogs, from the very youngest to the very oldest. They will all play with you if you start a game. Dogs love play so much they will amuse themselves with solitary games if no one is around to start a game.

The most playful activities for dogs are walking, retrieving sticks or balls, or anything that involves hiding objects. Whatever games you can devise, they are sure to be received with enthusiasm by your dog. Games involving a tossed ball or Frisbee are great fun for a dog because chasing something or jumping up to catch it are natural canine behaviors. Try to find a thick, indestructible dog toy designed for rough play. Not only will your dog chase and retrieve anything that bounces, he will enjoy dropping and chasing the toy when you are not there to throw it to him.

There are many types of balls to choose from, but the best for dogs are hard rubber balls. The ball should be large enough that the puppy cannot accidentally swallow it. Frisbees are fine for tossing in the air to catch because they are lightweight and large. Balls should never be tossed in the air to be caught; they are very hard and could crack a tooth or scare a young puppy on impact. Tennis balls should never be left with pups, who could skin or chew them into pieces that could then be swallowed. Rubber or cloth tug toys encourage your puppy to play tug-of-war and should be avoided. Never apply extreme resistance against your puppy's front teeth. This could alter his bite and affect the alignment of his teeth and jaw.

At no time should you allow the puppy's enthusiasm to get out of control. Any signs of aggression or attempts to snap or bite your hand should not be tolerated. Common sense should tell you when the dog is no longer playing a game. You must be able to end it without a fight and when you choose. If you feel that your puppy's behavior with a tug toy is beyond play and perhaps too aggressive, remove the toy until you get advice from your breeder or from a professional trainer.

Most dogs love hide-and-seek games and, because of their intelligence, are capable of building a large game vocabulary. By naming different objects or toys, you can easily teach your dog to find things that you have hidden. This is a game that will provide years of fun for both of you and can come in handy if you choose to enter tracking tests or if you simply misplace your keys.

Games you should avoid with your puppy are ones that cause him to become boisterous or promote aggressive behavior. Pushing, shoving, or play boxing games may start out to be fun but can turn ugly when your puppy starts growling and using his teeth. The usual response to being nipped or bitten is to smack the puppy, which in turn causes him to fear you and anything to do with the human hand. These games can end the possibility of developing a successful bond and are also destructive to the puppy's good nature. Ask yourself why you would ever want to encourage your best friend to use his teeth on you. And if he needs to protect you in the future against a robber or mugger, do you want him to back down because he's afraid of being hit? Even worse, do you want him to flinch with fear of your hands when you try to pet him?

Many dogs and their families enjoy the competition of dog shows, obedience trials, tracking tests, hunting tests, agility (competitive obstacle courses), and fly-ball (relay races with a caught ball). These are sports that, depending on how the dog is treated, provide a great deal of fun but can also play a large role in creating a bond. It is best for everyone, especially the dog, if these sports are viewed as pleasurable activities. With that as your goal, there are only winners.

Dog training is a wonderful bonding activity that teaches your pet how to live successfully in the human environment. It is quite clear, however, that an important side benefit of obedience training is bonding. When you obedience-train your dog, you develop the ability to control him. The process for doing this involves close, personal contact and direct communication between you and the dog. These are the essential ingredients for creating the emotional bond that is so necessary for a lasting relationship.

The dog training offered in this course uses motivational techniques based on rewards and corrections. When using these training techniques properly, you must communicate with your pet on a meaningful level. You are required to convey to him your approval when he does the right thing and your disapproval when he does the wrong thing.

The teaching process of dog training involves talking, touching, socializing, and in a sense, playing. Whenever the dog does the right thing, he is lavishly praised and given a great deal of encouragement. When he does not obey, he is given a correction, which may be a tug of the leash or a firm verbal reprimand. Both aspects of training involve communication, which is precisely what is required to create a bond with your dog. Even when house-breaking your dog, you should make a big fuss over him when he relieves himself in the right place. He must be walked and given his food and water on a frequent schedule. He must be confined to one area. He must be corrected for mistakes. These are all close-contact activities that create an involvement between the dog and his family and help set the bond.

Your puppy will get into mischief that makes you laugh, such as going into the bathroom and stealing toilet paper, and these scenes can become part of the bonding process. Tell him *No,* and then give him lavish praise for obeying you by stopping. You can bond with your dog by talking to him as you feed him. "Hey, here comes dinner. Here's chow, puppy." The puppy will gaze at you as you communicate.

You can bond with your dog as you medicate him with eyedrops or eardrops by trying to make it fun or by soothing his anxiety. You can bond when you groom him. Every time you touch your dog, you can talk to him and make it a happy occasion. Massaging your dog creates a feeling of relaxation for both of you as well as a feeling of physical communication.

"So, Gretchen and Wally, do you get the concept?"

Wally answers, "Well, Uncle Matty, it seems that you have to be pretty open with your feelings to do this. Right?"

"Right. Is that going to be a problem?"

Gretchen chimes in quickly, "Only if you have trouble showing your feelings to a dog."

Matty shakes his head.

"If you have trouble showing your feelings to a dog, then maybe you should consider a goldfish."

All the bonding activities available to you are meant to be pleasant, practical, and rewarding. Bonding with your dog does not take a whole lot of effort and it happens pretty quickly. For some it takes fifteen minutes. Whether it happens quickly or slowly, the bond lasts for a lifetime.

Three
Powerful Words

I'd like you to meet two new dog owners who share a Cairn Terrier puppy named Toto. Yes, it's the same breed as the dog in *The Wizard of Oz*. It's the little one that Judy Garland kept hugging. I knew you'd ask. These women are worried about the damage that their five-month-old dog can do to their valuable possessions because he's not trained. Dorothy Dougherty and Georgia King are partners in an antiques business in Boston and each relates to their new dog in her own way. When people living with the same dog have different personalities, they usually have contrasting reactions to the dog's behavior, and this confuses the little guy because he gets mixed messages. Georgia and Dorothy work together, live together, and get along very well, but they are very different people. Their antiques business on Beacon Street is very successful, and they want to be able to keep the dog in the store, which is loaded with expensive furniture and carpets that could easily be ruined by the puppy, who just doesn't know right from wrong yet.

"Okay, who wants to talk first?"

Dorothy, a tall, attractive woman in her early forties with lots of energy, holds the dog.

She says in a firm tone of voice, "That would be me."

"Okay."

Matty reaches out to the little bundle of hair squirming every which way to get free from her arms and kisses his nose.

She continues with uncertainty, "This is a great dog, at least I think he's a great dog, but he has already peed on the satin upholstery of an expensive Victorian sofa, and now we don't have a prayer of selling it. He also put little teeth marks into the legs of a very expensive armoire, which is also unsaleable because of him. The dog needs discipline."

"All the dog needs is a rubber chew toy," responds her partner, Georgia.

Georgia is the smaller of the two women and a lot more relaxed. She smiles and pats Dorothy's arm.

"The teeth marks on the armoire legs are so small they actually make the piece look older and more valuable."

Dorothy shakes her head.

"You'll excuse anything this little guy does, won't you? As far as you're concerned, he can pee anywhere he wants. You're not going to be satisfied until he turns the whole shop into the yellow brick road. He's thinks he's the Wizard of Us. But he's just a wizzer."

Matty looks puzzled.

"A wizzer? What's a wizzer?"

Dorothy frowns, "A wizzer is a dog who keeps wizzing on our expensive furniture."

Georgia answers, "You're not in Kansas anymore, Dorothy. Lighten up. It's not that bad."

Dorothy shakes her head and puts the dog on the ground.

"Not that bad? Our little wizard cost us $3,500 in furniture. Are you crazy?"

I like these women. They're interesting and nice to work with. They are both bright, literate, and have a good sense of humor. Dorothy, the taller one, is a bit hawkish and strong-willed, and she doesn't back off from anything, especially an opinion. She gives no slack even if she's proved wrong. But despite her stubborn nature and aggressive manner, she's a very sweet person, deep down. Very deep down.

Georgia is fun because she doesn't take anything too seriously. To her everything is okay. It doesn't matter. She is very easygoing. She isn't bothered by Toto's destruction. In these two ladies you can see how opposites attract, which is probably why their business does so well. They own a high-profile shop that is a successful haunt of the local celebrities in Boston. Since Dorothy and Georgia travel quite a bit, when they first got their dog they were concerned with how fair it would be for the dog. They weren't sure if they had the time for a four-legged child with a tail. Now that they have the dog, they love him madly but he drives them crazy. I see them at their shop, where they spend most of their time, and they are anxious for Toto to stay there without doing damage. They don't want Toto to keep having accidents on the furniture. And Toto has other problems, too. He growls and bites them. The dog is a strong-willed and hardheaded puppy. What can I say, he's a terrier.

"Okay, ladies, here's the deal. What you have is a typical

puppy with all the usual puppy problems. And if you think about it, they aren't really problems."

"What do you mean, Matthew?" asked Dorothy in an abrupt tone of voice.

"Toto is a puppy and he's doing what puppies do. He has to relieve himself and doesn't know where to do it. He wants the comfort he got from his mother, so he likes the softness of the couches. And he's upset about being hollered at one minute, and then coddled the next. So he growls and nips. He's probably teething, too."

"It's bad, isn't it?" asked Dorothy, already convinced.

Georgia shakes her head.

"Dorothy, leave the dog alone. You're always picking on him."

"What? Me? Picking on him? That's not true, Georgia."

Matthew steps in.

"Hold it. Time out. You're both right and you're both wrong. Dorothy, he's just a puppy and simply needs to be obedience-trained. He just doesn't know what you want him to do. You've got to stop hollering at him. Not so fast, Georgia. You're just as much at fault here, too. You're too soft on the guy. He needs to be taught what to do and then have the two of you make him do the right thing. That means you, too, Ms. Softee. Between the two of you the dog is going to go nuts. Once we get this dog obedience-trained most of his problems are going to disappear. Now I'm going to set up a housebreaking program for you, but what the dog needs the most is obedience training. Okay?"

The women nod reluctantly.

"Now, what I want you to do is just listen while I discuss a very important part of dog training. I want you to learn to use the words *No* and *Okay* properly, to use a leash and collar as training tools, and I want you to learn how to correct the dog with a leash correction. Now just listen. This is not the time for my cutesy Uncle Matty voice."

Two Powerful Words

Now, pay attention. *No* is a command to stop a dog from doing something wrong, such as stealing food, peeing on the floor, or hopping up on the sofa when you don't want him there. *No* is a correction and only requires the one word rather than a string of sentences that the dog doesn't understand anyway. Dogs become confused when their owners do not say the precise words of a specific command or give mixed messages. If Dorothy is tough in her manner and Georgia is permissive in her manner, then the dog is either going to become confused or learn how to play one owner off the other. Dogs are like kids. Once they see a conflict between parents, they automatically work the situation to their advantage. And then everybody gets upset.

How the commands are said adds to a dog's understanding of them and what they mean. If you two don't have a concept of dog training, you'll say just about anything to get Toto to stop his bad behavior. It'll come out as "Knock it off", "Cut it out!", "Stop! Stop! Stop!", or "Toto, if you don't stop it this minute, I'm gonna smack you." When you tell a dog that he's bad or should be ashamed, you are communicating to him that you no longer approve or even like him and that eats away at the carefully created bond you developed with him.

The command *No* is a blessing because it cannot be interpreted as anything but a red light for bad behavior. It is a negative message and is one of those words that sounds just like what it means. It's a showstopper. There is no way to say *No* and confuse the dog, unless, of course, you sound like Georgia! Even a child can get a dog to stop what he's doing with *No,* if it is said with just the least bit of conviction. The dog will always associate *No* with your displeasure and stop what he's doing instantly if you convey to him that he has actually done the wrong thing. If you use this one word consistently in appropriate situations, you can turn his behavior around. By using the word properly and at the right time, you will create an automatic response to your demand that will work every time.

"Ladies, please pay attention to what I'm about to say because this is important. Never give the command *No* with the dog's name anywhere near that word. It would be a shame to create a bad association with his name. There are negative consequences if you make him feel bad every time you use his name, especially in the action commands such as *Heel.*

"You know, Dorothy, I have the impression that you're the one doing this."

She protests defensively.

"Me? Why would you think that?"

"Well, I noticed that when you call the dog by his name he won't go near you."

"Well, that's because the little stinker hates me."

Georgia chimes in.

"No. He doesn't hate you. He's just a little scared of you."

"Scared of me? Why?"

Georgia smiles.

"Are you kidding? We're *all* scared of you."

"Wait a minute. Before this becomes an encounter group, can I get back to the subject of *No* as an important command word, please? Just listen, okay?"

When commanding your dog to walk in *Heel,* you must say the dog's name before giving the command word. Saying his name not only gets the dog's attention, it alerts him to the idea that he is going to be in motion: "Toto, *Heel,*" "Toto, *Come.*" Imagine calling Toto to you to hear you say, "Toto, you peed on the sofa again, you rotten little stinker." No dog in his right mind is going to respond to his name if it is used for something unpleasant. Just say the word by itself. By simply saying *No* you can correct a dog and get him to stop whatever wrong behavior he's doing without any other words.

It is also important to remember that you should never use the command *No* more than once with each correction. One well-said *No* gets the job done without a string of commands, sentences, or actions. It also stops you from getting upset with your dog. In this way, dogs are like people. They do not want to be bullied by your anger or excessive authority as you give them obedience commands. "No, no, no," said over and over again with anger and frustration will upset any dog and make the dog frightened of you as well. A firm, vocal sound, spoken clearly, without hesitation, and with self-confidence, gets the right response from the dog. Take a few seconds before giving a command like *No.* Breathe in deeply and force the air way down into your stomach. As you release the air say, *No.* You will get an immediate improvement in the clarity and tone of your voice, which will resonate with a deeper sound. A self-confident voice will deliver the message to the dog that there's a new game in town and it's called *I give the commands, you obey them.*

Remember, all you really want to do is get your dog's attention and get him to understand that he just did something wrong, or did something incorrectly. Now, this isn't a federal crime. So don't scare him or make him pee on the spot because you thundered *No* in a way that makes him feel guilty. The correction *No* should only tell him that he is doing something wrong. It's just communication, that's all.

On the other hand, you don't want to be a wuss either, with a manner that's too mild or a weak voice. No whining or nagging, please. Most dogs are clever and learn very quickly how gullible their family is. They figure out how to manipulate humans into letting them get away with murder. The loss of the dog's love and affection is a constant worry for some people. But you know what? The love and respect from a dog comes from being trained and understanding who is in charge and what is expected. Dogs are grateful to know, once and for all, what they should and should not do. The various commands involved in dog training define the relationship between the dog and his family. When the dog knows how to please his family he becomes happy and content because it is his nature to live in harmony. If he were living in a dog or wolf pack in the wild, he would need to get along by accepting his rank, doing his job, and pleasing those above him within the pack. When you incorporate love and affection into your dog's training, he will return the favor by obeying your commands faithfully and offering something a lot like love in return. Praise is his reward. Verbal and leash corrections tell him when he has made a mistake and motivate him to please you. Most dogs want to please and work for praise. It is a form of approval and they crave it.

How to Use No Properly

"Now, Dorothy, I know I've been hard on you, but this subject is especially important for you."

"And why is that, Uncle Matty?" she answers sarcastically.

"Uh oh. You're upset and I haven't even said anything yet."

Georgia comes to her friend's defense.

"Well, really, Matthew, Dorothy loves the dog as much as I do, you know."

"You're right. I'm going to approach this from another angle. Georgia, this is especially important for *you,* considering the kinds of mistakes *you* make with Toto."

Georgia's eyes widen with surprise.

"Mistakes? What mistakes? I'm the one that's really good with this dog."

"Hold it. Just listen to what I have to say, please, and try not to act like you're fourteen. It's nothing personal. It's just business."

"Where have I heard *that* before?" says Georgia.

"You, my dear, are extremely lax with Toto. Whatever he does is fine with you."

"So what's wrong with that?"

"Nothing—if you want to watch your customers fly out of your store whenever they see urine-stained furniture for sale and a floor that you won't find in the Emerald City. Your Good Witch of the East act doesn't work. Letting the dog get away with everything isn't doing him or anyone else any favors."

Georgia gets angry.

"Well, her Wicked Witch of the West can't be any good. How can anyone be hard on a little dog like Toto?"

"Georgia, Georgia. Calm down. Take a breath, count to seventeen."

"Seventeen?"

"Would you prefer ten? Come on, now. Don't be mad. I'm just saying that with the right training and by introducing the commands *No* and *Okay* you both will have proper control over your dog. It's absolutely necessary. Trust me."

Although saying the command *No* is not very complicated, it is important to know when to say it, how to say it, and what to do immediately after you say it. First, you have to consider *No* as a command word and not some informal comment about how you feel. Use this command as a correction whenever and wherever the dog is either incorrectly obeying a command, such as *Down* or *Stay,* or has decided not to obey at all. In either case, you have to let him know that you're unhappy with his behavior or lack of performance. The command *No* says all that to him. Besides being a command, *No* is also the verbal part of a correction, with or without the use of a leash. *No* also stops negative behavior, such as jumping on people or running out the door, and it should stop it immediately.

"Did I mention that you must not use his name with the correction?"

Both women chime in together.

"Several times, Uncle Matty. We get it."

"All right. All right. Just checking. It's important enough to repeat."

Dorothy says, "Are you aware of how much you repeat yourself? I think I'm with my Uncle Al who's in the Old Actors Home."

"Thank you very much for sharing that. Now please pay attention. Uncle Matty may be proud, but he's *not* Uncle Al."

Some dogs respond instantly to the command *No* while others take three or four seconds. Always give your dog the benefit of the doubt by allowing him enough time to respond. You may have noticed that some breeds are much faster in their responses than others. You should never have to say *No* more than once, assuming the dog has been trained. Immediately following the command *No,* praise your dog for obeying you. This is really important. If the dog has responded satisfactorily, praise him to the moon and the stars. Remember, praise is the motivator. Your dog will work for it, I promise you. Also, bear in mind that it is your tone of voice that makes him obey you, not necessarily the word itself. It's the way you say it that counts. Bring the sound up from way down in the pit of your stomach. Take in a deep, deep breath. Take in enough air so the sides of your waist expand. As you exhale, say *No* in as deep a sound as possible. You will be amazed how different your voice will sound. Your voice will have so much authority, you can then get a job reading news on the radio. Try practicing this as much as possible. It's worth it. If the dog does not respond to you when you say *No,* then there is something wrong with the way you're saying it. Go back to the deep-breathing exercise and try to be as firm as possible without scaring the dog.

One last thought about corrections and use of the command *No*. Never hit your dog, not for any reason. Hitting teaches your dog nothing, and it only makes him fear you as it quickly destroys the bond you have established. There is no place for abuse when you live with a dog. *No* is a powerful word that corrects your dog without punishing him. It is a precise word that does the job. You will no doubt use it as a correction throughout your dog's life. It is very useful as long as it is not misused.

Using *Okay* Properly

"Georgia, is it okay if I direct this at Dorothy? I mean, you're not going to get bent out of shape, are you?"

"Now what?" says Dorothy.

"Well, just as Georgia has to learn how to say *No* more often, you could use some practice being positive with your dog. And there is nothing more positive than the word *Okay*."

"You know, I'm not sure I like this."

"Dorothy, I'm here to help you and help the dog. I have to be honest about what I see or I'm of no use to you. Most dog problems are essentially people problems. All I'm saying is that the dog is fine and isn't as bad as you think. He's a baby and just needs to be trained. But more importantly, he has to feel that you are not always mad at him. Just be more positive around him, and with me training the dog everything will be fine, and we'll all go to the seashore. Okay?"

"Is Uncle Matty proud? If you're not proud, I'll be crushed."

"Uncle Matty's *soooo* proud!"

"Okay, then. Let's get on with it. *Okay*, you say?"

"Yes."

The command *Okay* is the ultimate verbal approval because it not only tells your dog that you love him, but it also tells him that school's out for the day. *Okay* is also a release from some commands like having to walk by your side in *Heel*. You're walking down the street and your trained dog is obeying the command *Heel* by keeping his head even with your left leg. He is allowed to leave that fixed position and relieve himself wherever it's acceptable—if you give him permission with the command word *Okay*, said with happiness and exuberance as you immediately slacken the leash. Believe me, he'll know what to do. Your exuberance triggers his motion. This word is also part of several action commands that result in forward motion. "*Okay*, Jamie. *Heel*." "*Okay*, Lucy. *Come*. *Okay*!" (If said with enthusiasm, the dog leaves her position and runs to the end of the leash to get to the street to relieve himself.) *Okay* can be used by itself to release the dog. It can also be an affirmative prefix to his name as part of another command.

The command is positive in its application and even in its sound. When used properly, *Okay* tells the dog that something nice is happening. In addition to being a release from training, it is also an important part of the command *Come When Called*. This is the command you use to call the dog to you from a distance. When using *Come When Called* you must raise your voice to call your dog to you if he is not close or he won't hear you. But when you yell at your dog, your voice could sound like you're hollering at him and that might make him hesitate. It could sound like you're saying, "Get your tail over here or I'm gonna give you what for." Now think about the word *Okay*. It's a positive word that is a lot like "yes." If you put it in front of a command, it sounds very positive. "*Okay*, Toto, come," is a lot friendlier than "Toto, get over here before I have a heart attack." *Okay* is hard to say with a bad meaning attached to it. The word seems to have a happy sound built into it, maybe because of the *O* part of the word. It always goes up in a cheerful way, forcing your voice to go higher. *Okay* will always suggest to your dog that everything is good.

The most important thing about using *Okay* is to be sure you only use it when everything *is* okay. A negative use of the word will make it ineffective in a very short time. Its use as a training tool will be over. Despite the fact that *Okay* is an upbeat, happy-sounding word, it is still a command word in the sense that it gets the dog ready for action. When the dog hears *Okay*, he responds in a special way, just like any other command.

Teaching *Okay* as a Release

This is easy. If you walk your housebroken dog on-leash so he can relieve himself at a designated place outdoors, this command will be very helpful. A dog that knows how to obey the command *Heel* knows that he must walk to the left of his owner's side. There should only be approximately three feet of the leash draped across the front of the owner's legs. The remainder of the leash is gathered up in the owner's hand. This tight leash control prevents the dog from weaving from side to side as they walk together. Once you get to the place where it is acceptable for the dog to go, say *Okay* in a pleasant tone of voice and let that part of the leash that is gathered up slip through your hands. This allows the dog to go directly to the spot he likes best. Usually, the dog goes directly to the right place, which should be in the street. It will not take long for the dog to understand what the procedure is if he is given this routine on a consistent basis. *Okay* will become a very important word for him.

Ending a training session is another way to use *Okay* as a release. "*Okay*, Toto, we're finished" is all you have to say and then stand back as your happy dog relaxes. *Okay* will be a welcome sound.

Some Training Tools You Will Need

"Now I don't want either of you to be insulted or hurt at my next comment."

Georgia and Dorothy pretend to brace themselves in exaggerated theatrical style.

"Oh, dear. He's gonna get us again. Watch it, Georgia. This Uncle Matty is a dangerous man."

"Come on. I have to talk to you about this leash you've got around your poor dog's neck. Now, no one understands the fashion statement involved in a paisley, three-foot-long leash as much as I do, especially if it's hooked onto a Tiffany silk scarf. Let's see. You probably have about $200, maybe $300, invested in this, right?"

Georgia squints at Matty with suspicion. She knows the punch line is coming.

"Yeah. So what?" she answers slowly.

"Well this is just great if you're going to keep your dog in a glass display case at Bloomingdale's. Of course, if you want your dog to be trained, to be walked, to be controlled, to be kept safe from traffic and all kinds of strangers, then you might want to consider a leash and collar that actually keeps him where you want him. But paisley and silk are okay with me if you want an eight-pound beast roaming around your store, doing what he wants, wherever he wants to do it."

"Okay, Uncle Matty. Tell us what we should have," says Dorothy.

"Say 'please.'"

She laughs.

"Please. Ooh. Pretty please."

"Smart aleck. You guys need to get a proper leash and collar for mighty Toto, here. Come here baby."

Matty picks up Toto and cradles him in his arms.

"Talk to Uncle Matty. Uncle Matty loves you."

Toto melts in his arms and licks his face as he continues the lesson.

The Leash

Before we can move into the next phase of training, the leash correction, also called the corrective jerk, there are some essential training tools you need to train your dog. You must have a leash and a collar. You cannot train your dog without them. I have always used a six-foot leather leash with a hand loop on one end and a metal clip at the other end. The leash is the primary tool for training dogs or dealing with their behavior problems. It is the most important training equipment you'll need, because it is necessary for teaching, correcting, and controlling the dog and in the long run can save his life.

Leashes are available in leather, braided nylon, smooth

nylon webbing, waxed cotton (Cordo-hyde), and metal chain. A six-foot leather leash is the safest, most durable type for training and for everyday use when you're taking your dog out for a walk. Leather softens with age, making it more comfortable for the dog and longer lasting than other materials, and is easier on your hands as well as on the dog's body. There is no way to know in advance when a metal chain leash is about to break, which is not the case with leather. As a leather leash begins to wear it thins out, so it is easy to see when it is time to replace it. Metal leashes sometimes develop sharp edges that can irritate or scratch the dog's body, and while nylon webbing is very popular because of its strength, light weight, and bright colors, it can irritate your hand if your dog pulls away from you very quickly.

When you pick a quality leather leash, get one that is five-eighths of an inch wide for a medium to large dog. This will provide needed strength for a large dog without over-whelming him if he is delicate or has a long coat. Wider widths can be used for very large dogs and narrower widths for small ones. A strong, comfortable leash should be your main concern when you shop for this essential item.

The Collar

You will also need a training collar, which is sometimes referred to as a choke collar. These are short lengths of chain or nylon with a large ring at each end. The best ones are made of small metal links that are welded together. By looping the chain through one of the large rings, you form a slipknot that is wide enough to slide over the dog's head and onto his neck.

Size is an important consideration as well. When the

collar is too long, it becomes too heavy for the dog and the leash corrections become ineffective. Measure the diameter of your dog's neck and purchase a chain or nylon collar that is three inches longer than your dog's neck size. The leash snaps onto the outer ring. It is best to get a nylon training collar for puppies, delicate dogs, and dogs with long, silky fur that is easily damaged.

The training or choke collar is the second most essential tool required for training a dog, after the leash. By learning how to put the collar on the dog's neck properly you will see how it works and why it is so effective. A choke collar is just a segment of chain links with a large metal ring at each end, but choke collars are also made of leather and nylon, both of which are as effective as metal collars. The leather and nylon collars are more useful for dogs with long fur because they don't wear away the hair around the dog's neck.

If you think about it, a choke collar is a lasso. It goes around a dog's neck and tightens with the pressure placed on it. A choke collar can be improvised by taking the hand loop that is at the end of most leashes and running the other end of the leash through it. Instead of hooking the metal clip of the leash to a collar, run it through the loop and you have a temporary lasso or choke collar, depending on how you need to use it. Place it around the dog's neck, hold the metal clip in your hand, and pull it gently until the loop tightens. This is very useful in an emergency if the real collar breaks or if your dog somehow gets away from you. You can use this improvised bit of equipment until you get your dog home and out of harm's way. This improvised lasso or choke collar is very effective for catching a dog that will not let you get a hold of him. Bear in mind that this should only be used as a temporary collar. Do not attempt to train your dog with an improvised choke collar. It could be dangerous, and it certainly won't work as well as one that is manufactured for that purpose.

The purpose of the choke collar is to communicate to the dog through a mild negative sensation plus a metallic sound message that he did the wrong thing. It must never be thought of or used as a punishment device. The training collar is a correction device and it does not hurt the dog.

The way to use the collar properly is to attach it to a six-foot leather leash. If you use it properly, you pull the leash to the side, causing the collar to gently tighten around the dog's neck for a split second. You must then release the tension of the leash immediately so the collar loosens right away. If the collar has been placed around the dog's neck correctly, it will loosen around the neck instantly. If it is not on correctly, it will remain tight around the neck even though you have released the tension from the leash. Remember: Verbal praise must always follow such a correction.

In my opinion, nothing is more effective, kinder, or humane than a training collar. It is easier on a dog than a very harsh tone of voice and far more communicative. Without it you couldn't train a dog properly or solve many of the behavior problems that spring up in the life of a dog. One reasonably firm leash correction using the leather leash and the metal choke collar, and the dog immediately understands not to do whatever he did that was wrong. It is far more effective and ultimately kinder than standing next to a disobedient dog repeating *No* or *Down* or *Sit* over and over again. Where's the kindness in that? Next to a leash, the choke collar is the dog owner's most valuable tool.

Once you position the collar correctly, it becomes the easiest thing to do thereafter. Let the collar hang down in a vertical position as you hold it by the large ring with your left hand. The collar automatically falls into a vertical strip. Take hold of the large ring at the bottom of the chain with your right hand. Maneuver the bottom of the chain through the bottom ring so it begins to form a loop. Allow the chain to drop through the bottom ring, which will happen because of its weight and because of gravity. This will create a slipknot that can go around your dog's neck.

Next, place the collar over your dog's neck. The ring in your left hand should point away from the dog's right side. You are doing it correctly if it looks like the letter *P* (for perfect) around the dog's neck. If it is incorrect, the collar resembles the number *9* on the left and number *6* on the right and it will not slide back and forth. The collar must tighten around the dog's neck when pulled to the side and loosen when released. It is of vital importance for the dog's comfort and safety that the collar slide back and forth smoothly and quickly.

With the collar correctly placed around the dog's neck, clip the leash to the outstanding large ring that is dangling down the side. Like any slipknot, the chain will tighten around the dog's neck when the leash is pulled gently. When the collar is tightened, the dog will experience a mild sensation. If the word *No* always accompanies this mild sensation, the dog will learn that he has not per-

The correct position forms the letter **P.**

Photo by Jonathan Alcorn/Zuma.

The incorrect position forms the number 9 or the number 6.

Photo by Jonathan Alcorn/Zuma.

formed properly. It is a negative message. Release the leash immediately after pulling it so the collar does not stay tightened around the dog's neck.

About the Leash Correction

Since your dog does not speak, you have to wonder how you're going to tell him that he's done the right or the wrong thing. It isn't really something you have to tell him as much as communicate to him. There are two basic things to which he will respond: your approval and your disapproval. So how do you communicate either one of these two things to him? Assuming you have established a good bond between you and your dog, it is only natural for him to accept the concept that he must obey the commands you give, once he has learned them. If he refuses to obey a command, or if he performs it incorrectly, he must somehow become aware of your disapproval. Hollering at or hitting him may get across the idea that he was wrong, but then his mind will not be in any condition to go to the next step, which is to correct the situation and do the right thing. What can he possibly learn from a smack other than fear of you and your hands? The only things you should ever do to your dog with your hands is teach him, nurture him, and express your love for him.

The most effective technique for correcting a dog's behavior and communicating your disapproval is the leash correction, also known as the corrective jerk. The leash correction is one of the most important training techniques in this obedience course and will be used throughout. Once you learn how to properly execute this technique, you will have at your disposal a way of communicating to your dog that cuts through all the doubts. When you are dissatisfied with his performance and demand that he do better, you need only give him a leash correction and he will know immediately that he must improve. This technique is so valuable as a teaching and communicating tool that you will use it throughout the life of your dog.

The first leash correction you give your dog will get his attention, but it will also be a big surprise as well. If you do it properly, it will definitely not hurt him but it will shake him up. For the first time your dog will know in clear terms that he displeased you. Because the technique calls for a firmly stated *No,* there is little doubt in the dog's mind that he has done something wrong. From then on he will continue to learn your right from his wrong. The idea is to give your dog a leash correction whenever he does not execute a command properly or does anything that you feel he shouldn't be doing. The leash correction, or corrective jerk, can upset the dog if you do not praise your dog lavishly immediately after each jerk of the leash. After each and every correction you must praise your dog so he understands that you are still friends. The praise is also a verbal reward for accepting the correction and doing the right thing.

It is important to understand that administering one firm leash correction is much more effective than giving the dog five or ten jerks that are too mild or too timid. Little ineffective corrections not only fail to do the job, they end up irritating and tiring the dog much more than one proper correction. You can also render the technique useless if you use it excessively and for unimportant reasons. The dog will become weary of it and confused. If you say

No firmly each time you correct the dog, you will eventually eliminate the need to jerk the leash. Your spoken correction, *No,* will elicit the proper response. Eventually, the leash correction will create an automatic response in him each time you say *No,* and it will last throughout the dog's life.

Before Correcting the Dog, Hold the Leash Properly

Attach the six-foot leather leash to the dog's training collar. Place the thumb of your right hand through the top loop of the leash. Stand to the dog's right, so both of you face the same direction. With your left hand, bring the middle of the leash over to the right, wrapping it around your right thumb over the loop. In effect, you will have three straps of leather across the palm of your right hand. Close the fingers of your right hand around the three straps with your fingernails facing you. Adjust the length of the leash so it crosses no more than the width of your body, allowing just a few inches of slack. Half the leash should be in your right hand, while half hangs loosely between your right hand, across your knees, and onto the dog's collar. Close the fingers of your right hand and clench the leash firmly with your palm facing up. Place your left hand under your right, clench the leash strands with your left palm facing down for reinforcement of the grip. Gripping the folded leash with your left hand as well will give you added security. When you position your left hand directly under the right, both hands are holding the leash like a baseball bat. The fingers of your left hand should be pointing away from your body. Both hands hold the leash, but in opposite directions. This gives you the most secure grip possible and allows you to administer a proper leash correction.

Only two or three feet of the leash should extend from the dog's collar across the front of your knees. The remainder of the leash should dangle from your hands, barely touching the outer right thigh. You now have a firm hold and absolute control. If the dog tries to get away from you, your thumb will keep the leash firmly in your hand.

Once the length of the leash is correct for both you and your dog, draw a line with a felt-tip marker on the middle portion of the leash where it loops over your thumb. This will help you find the correct place on the leash every time.

How to Administer a Leash Correction

How you give the correction depends on the dog's age; size; physical strength; sensitivity; and temperament. Common sense is the best guide. Obviously, a small, delicate dog like Toto cannot, and should not, be jerked very hard, if at all. The same is true for a dog that is shy or very sensitive. Puppies require special consideration. But the average dog with an even temperament should be corrected firmly.

Once a dog has demonstrated that he has learned what you have taught him, it is fair to correct him if he does not obey or does the wrong thing. In dog training, he must respond on command. If your dog does not respond properly, you should give him a mild correction using the leash correction.

Attach the leash to the dog's collar and face the same

Place the thumb of your right hand in the loop at the top of the leash. Bring the middle of the leash over to the right, wrapping it around the thumb over the loop. Place your left hand under your right, clenching the leash strands with both hands. With your left hand directly under the right, both hands are holding the leash like a baseball bat.

Photos by Jonathan Alcorn/Zuma.

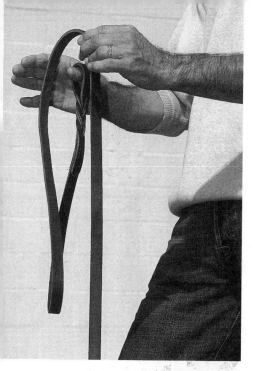

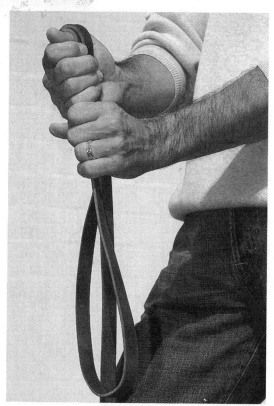

direction as the dog. The dog should be standing or sitting by your left side. Always stand by the dog's right side for the sake of consistency. Be certain approximately two or three feet of the leash is draped across your legs. Grip

Face the same direction as the dog with the dog at your left side. Drape two or three feet of the leash across your legs. Hold the leash with both hands a bit below waist level. Jerk the leash sideways and slightly upward to the right. Photos by Jonathan Alcorn/Zuma.

the leash firmly as described before. This will give you just enough leash to pull upward and to your right in a quick, snapping motion. Hold the leash with both hands a bit below waist level. Jerk the leash sideways and slightly upward to the right. When the leash is jerked, the training collar tightens around the dog's neck, giving him a mild sensation. As you jerk the leash say *No* in a firm tone of voice. Return to the original position. Do not jerk a puppy or sensitive dog too hard. As your hands quickly return to their original position, the collar should automatically loosen. It is essential for the dog's well-being that the collar loosens immediately. If it does not, then it is around the dog's neck incorrectly.

Once the dog has responded to the leash correction and has obeyed your command or stopped an offensive action, you must praise him generously. Let your dog know that he has pleased you. It is important to encourage a dog by praising him every step of the way.

When teaching yourself how to execute the corrective jerk, do not practice on the dog. It will exhaust him and create confusion. The correction is merely a tool to be used when teaching the other commands. It is not an end in itself. It would make a lot more sense to practice on a broom handle or stairway banister until you have learned to execute the maneuver correctly.

Leash Corrections for Dogs of Different Temperaments

If your dog has a High-Energy temperament, use a firm, authoritative tone of voice with a strong correction with the leash. Do not scare him, just be authoritative.

If your dog has a Shy temperament, use a soft tone of voice, as though you were speaking to a child. When correcting him, tug on the leash in a very gentle manner.

A dog with a Strong-Willed temperament should be corrected very firmly when necessary. Administer the leash correction in a determined, quick manner. Use a firm tone of voice. Be authoritative and execute a no-nonsense correction. Do not scare your dog, though. Even a Strong-Willed dog may simply not understand the basics of the command. Give him the benefit of the doubt and repeat the teaching portion of the command.

If your dog is Easygoing, use a demanding yet encouraging tone of voice. Try to be slightly authoritative without upsetting him. When correcting him be firm, command his attention, but use a mild correction

If your dog is Dominant-Aggressive, adjust the intensity of your voice correction to the size, age, and degree of aggressiveness of the dog. A dog with a Dominant-Aggressive temperament might snap or bite if the tone of your voice is too harsh or challenging. Be firm and authoritative without scaring him. If your Dominant-Aggressive dog is a puppy between seven weeks and six months of age, use a firm tone of voice. If your Dominant-Aggressive dog is between six months and ten months of age, use a very firm tone of voice. Without actually shouting or hollering, make sure the dog understands that you mean business by the sound of your voice. A Dominant-Aggressive dog that is older than ten months of age may be too difficult to handle. Have the dog evaluated by a professional dog trainer, animal behaviorist, or veterinarian.

The Dominant-Aggressive dog requires that you use the leash according to the demands of the dog and the situation. For puppies between the ages of seven weeks and six months, execute firm leash corrections. They should be administered in a manner that establishes you as the dominant figure. You must win in each situation where the young dog challenges your authority, although not at the expense of the dog's well-being. The corrective jerk is not meant to be abusive in any way. The idea is to teach the dog his behavioral boundaries, not to punish him. For young dogs between the ages of six months and ten months, use very firm and authoritative leash corrections. Do not back down in any leash correction situation unless the dog is becoming very aggressive. In that event, seek professional help. Once the dog is past ten months of age, you must have him evaluated by a professional before attempting to train him.

If your dog is Fear-Aggressive, voice corrections are important. Fear-Aggressive dogs are, in a sense, shy, and they behave aggressively with those who frighten them. This behavior is purely defensive in nature. The improper use of your voice could cause such a dog to bite. A seven-week- to six-month-old puppy requires gentler handling. He must be allowed to be a puppy, although corrections are essential. Give him firm but not harsh voice corrections. If the dog is six months to ten months old, use your voice in a firm, authoritative manner. A Fear-Aggressive dog that is older than ten months of age may be too difficult to handle. Have the dog evaluated by a professional dog trainer, animal behaviorist, or veterinarian.

The Fear-Aggressive dog must be handled in a slightly different manner. You must take into account the shy, frightened part of his temperament. A seven-week- to six-month-old puppy requires leash corrections that are not severe. Be firm, but use a softer touch when jerking the leash. If the dog is six months to ten months old, use a firm, authoritative tug of the leash when administering a corrective jerk. A Fear-Aggressive dog that is older than ten months of age is difficult to handle. Have the dog evaluated by a professional dog trainer, animal behaviorist, or veterinarian.

"Okay, ladies. Are we clear?"

Matty says it louder.

"Are we clear?"

Both Dorothy and Georgia move in close to Matty as though they were ganging up on him.

"So, Matty. Are you saying that Toto is a Dominant-Aggressive dog, or a Fear-Aggressive dog, or what?" asks Dorothy, using her height to tower over Matthew.

"Well, Dorothy. Toto is a lot like you."

"And what does that mean?"

"He's no Twinky, kid. If I were you, I'd read this chapter carefully, if you want to get him under control. And then I'd read the rest of the book. Uncle Matty's proud. Can I go now?"

Four
Be Seated

SIT

Some people believe that all they have to do is snap out a command to get their dog to do something and, as if by magic, the dog will do what they want. In *The Music Man*, Professor Harold Hill, a traveling con artist, sells the town of River City musical instruments for a marching band based on his Think System. His system relied on learning anything by simply thinking it. Well, my friends, if you rely on the Think System to get your dog trained you've got trouble, trouble right here in River City. When it comes to dog training, don't even think about it. Dogs are a lot like children. If you don't teach them what to do, they can't do it. How is a dog supposed to obey your commands without even knowing what the command means? You can stand there yelling your heart out—sit . . . Sit . . . *SIT* . . . **SIT!!!** Dog training is about learning to communicate with your dog and, of course, understanding what needs to be communicated. How often have we seen a dog owner snap out a command to an obedient dog that responded perfectly and assume that the dog simply understood what the owner said? What doesn't occur to many of us is how the dog knows what to do. It's not magic. It's dog training.

At this moment, I am outside a beautiful white stucco house in the heart of San Francisco. I'm on Divisadero Street, not too far from Twin Peaks, and I'm telling you it's not only attractive, it's fascinating. Every sixty minutes a sightseeing bus goes by loaded with tourists who wave at us. I can't tell if they're waving at the family standing next to me or their dog. Every time the noisy bus drives by the dog goes into a perfect Sit position and stares at it. Of course, the dog won't sit when you tell him to do it. But how could he? He's never been trained. The people who live here own a ten-month-old herding dog, a Welsh corgi, Pembroke (the breed without the tail), and he's named Foster. Corgis are little dogs with powerful personalities. Foster is smart, too. I like this little guy.

"The family that belongs to Foster is made up of Michael Bennett..."

"Hi. I'm the dad."

"Thanks, Dad, now please wait until I throw you a cue. Next is Lilly Bennett."

"Hello, I guess that makes me the mom."

"Do you mind waiting until I call you?"

"Sorry."

"Then there's Sally, their ten-year-old."

"Daughter, here."

"When did I lose control?"

Matty pauses, stares at the eight-year-old boy, and waves him over.

"Come on, you might as well introduce yourself."

The boy stands motionless. Matty waves again.

"Come on. Don't you want to say hello to everybody?"

The boy does not budge.

"Anyway, over there is Ben."

Finally Ben moves quickly to Matty's side.

"I'm eight."

"Thank you very much. Ben is eight."

"The dog is my brother."

Matty smiles and puts his arm around Ben.

"I like this boy. You know, Ben, I have a son, too. But he's a grown-up. Well, he thinks he's a grown-up. So Foster is your brother?"

"Yeah."

"Is he your younger brother or your older brother?"

"Don't be ridiculous, Mr. Margolis. The dog is only ten months old. He's not really my brother. He's a dog. It was just an expression. I didn't think you'd take it literally. I mean, I used the brother thing as a metaphor. You see . . ."

"Okay. Somebody help me, please. Are you sure you're eight?"

He turns to Lilly for help.

"Mom? You want to give me a hand here, please. Thanks, Ben. I'd love to go on with this but we've got a dog to train here. *Sit,* Ben, *Sit.* Anyway, now you've met the family and you've met the dog. And we're going to teach them the command *'Sit* today. Pay attention."

Obedience training consists of well-defined verbal commands and hand signals that have been taught to a dog by associating them with specific actions. Through a teaching process based on repetition and practice, dogs learn to respond properly to the commands and the people giving them. What reinforces the learning is the concept of rewards and corrections. Notice I didn't say punishments. It's really very simple. After you show the dog what to do and associate it with a verbal command or a hand signal, you reward him for doing it properly or correct him for doing it improperly. Praise is your dog's reward for doing the right thing and is usually given in the form of an enthusiastic verbal compliment, such as, "Good girl. What a good dog!" Sometimes it's a just a pat on the body. I like my Uncle Matty high-pitched tone of voice. Some dog trainers use food tidbits for this, but I rarely do except in very specific situations. An obedience-trained dog works for your praise, which he considers his reward. Praise tells him you are pleased with him and strengthens the learning process for each command. Praise should be given enthusiastically but must not be squandered. When you train your dog, be sure he's really earned the reward. That will make him work harder for your approval. Every time you praise your dog, you are teaching him to do whatever he did just before the reward was given. This can work against you if you praise a dog immediately after he barks, chews destructively, or behaves in some other unwanted way. If you try to calm down a dog or soothe him after he does something wrong, then you are teaching him to do the wrong thing. Think about it. He barks. You tell him "It's okay, boy." That would be rewarding him for barking. Don't do that.

When you correct a dog, you are giving him a message that he did not obey a command or execute it properly. The traditional correction is a jerk of the leash, which is attached to a training or choke collar. This communicates a painless, negative message because it is usually accompanied by an authoritative *No* from the trainer or the dog's owner.

You have heard all of this before, but it's so important that it's worth repeating. There must never be any pain or abuse resulting from this correction technique. It is simply a means of communicating to the dog that he did the wrong thing. A correction is a part of the teaching method, not a punishment. Punishment is not kind and it certainly is ineffective as a teaching method. If you learn when and how to effectively praise or correct your dog, you will have at your fingertips the primary means of communicating with him. Praise and correction together are the most important ways of telling your dog he did the right thing or the wrong thing. Okay, now that I have that said let's get to the business of *Sit.*

Each command you teach your dog has a specific set of uses, and it is important to be consistent with those uses so that you do not confuse your dog. For example, the command *Sit* is incorrect if used to stop a dog from doing something you don't like, such as barking, running, or jumping. None of these things have anything to do with the command *Sit.* The way the command works is that after you say the command, *Sit,* the dog sits erect with all his weight on his haunches. His body should be upright and his front legs are supposed to be straight and slant inward slightly at the top. The dog cannot make a transition from jumping on someone to going into a Sit position. He must first be stopped from jumping before he can be commanded to *Sit.* This requires the command *No.*

"Okay, who wants to talk to me about the command *Sit?* Sally?"

The young girl shakes her head.

"Talk to Ben. I'm sure he wants to go first."

Ben is about to come forward when his father steps in front of him.

"I think maybe I ought to be the first. But I already taught the dog how to Sit. Maybe we should move on to something a little more difficult."

Matty smiles.

"Everybody thinks his or her dog knows *Sit.* Foster here is a cute little guy and is ten months old. Okay, Michael, let me see what you know about *Sit.* You say you know *Sit.* And Lilly, too. We have the whole family here."

Matty pretends to shout to an imaginary audience.

"Okay, folks. This is *Doggie Lessons,* the family show. Just like piano lessons. We're all going to learn how to train Foster. Poor Foster. He's looking up and saying, 'Oh, man. Why me?' Okay, you said that Foster does *Sit* for you sometimes. Show me what you do to get him to do it. Michael, take the leash and let me see."

Michael takes the leash and looks uncomfortably at his wife and two children. He is on the spot.

"Foster, sit."

The little dog stands and looks at Michael for a minute before turning away. "Sit, Foster. SIT. SIT. Come on, damn it, SIT!"

"Michael, Michael, Michael. He heard you and he's not sitting. I don't think he's getting the message."

The tall, paunchy man is flustered and says, "Well, that's because you're here. He actually does it when you're not here."

"Oh, sure. In another room, when it's dark out, when the moon is in the third house of the sun and when Venus is rising. Then, and only then, will Foster sit on command, right? What we need is to teach Foster to sit whenever we give him the command, whether there are distractions or not, no matter where he is or when we give the command. *Sit* is a very important command. It's the introduction to obedience training. We have to start out positively. My definition of *Sit* is when you tell a dog to sit ten times in a row, he sits ten times in a row, no matter what. And of course you must always start without distractions. That's the secret of all this."

Michael nods his head but tries to avoid what Matty is telling him.

"I think you should show me what to do first, so I can show everybody else later on."

"Well, that's the problem, Michael. You've been showing them ever since you got Foster and you're not getting anywhere. That's why I have everybody here together at one time. Just relax, okay. This is not *Father Knows Best*. This is the *Family Needs to Know* show. The bottom line is that you're paying me a lot of money to train your dog and it better work, but it won't work unless I teach everyone here how to train the dog.

"Okay, Matty, but just remember who signs the checks," says the irritated man.

"I thought Lilly did."

Lilly steps in and pats her husband on the arm.

"Honey, this is a group thing. Let's all learn together."

Michael backs off.

Sally pipes in, "Right, Daddy. Mom's right."

The father answers, "All right, kids. Let's just relax. Okay, Matty, explain why it is so important that Foster learns the command *Sit*. What's the big deal?"

"Sure."

"When you're giving Foster medication, you need him to be still. If you want him to get on the vet's examining table, he needs to know *Sit.* If he's being groomed, you want him to be still. Those are simple things. How about if you open the car door and he runs out. That's when you want him to *Sit.* The same is true if you accidentally open the front door and he is about to run out. It's a way of being able to control him. It's like putting a child in a chair. If he's seated, he's out of harm's way. How can you put on his leash and collar for a walk or for training if he's moving away? These lessons are like preschool. That's what we're doing here. A dog should sit when you tell him. And it shouldn't be a yelling contest. It should be *Sit,* simply and quietly. It should always be an upbeat command. Now everybody in this family has different personalities and different tones of voices. So what I'm going to teach you in this lesson is how to teach your dog *Sit.* Basically, if you tell a dog to *Sit,* he should sit back on his haunches and sit there with his head up thinking, 'Hey I did that. I'm part of the Bennett family, look at me. Foster Bennett, he's doing okay. And everyone should clap their hands for him.'"

Michael says, "Sounds good. I suppose you're right. But I don't know about that high tone of voice stuff."

"Don't worry. I'll teach you how to do it."

"Let's get back to this lesson. This command is important because it is the first time that you are introducing a sense of obedience and conditioning to the dog. It's his first day in school and you want to be positive, whether you're teaching *Heel,* automatic *Sit, Sit-Stay, Come When Called* or *Down.* But *Sit* is the most useful command you'll have. Without it you really don't have anything. As I said, you can use it everywhere in the home; the front gate;

when people come up, in the car; at the vet. It's important to have the whole family here at once because I want you all to do the same thing with the dog. I want you all on the same page. We need to be consistent here. I don't want the dog to get different messages.

"We want to be fair to Foster, right? Come on. Let me hear you."

In unison, the family says, "We want to be fair to Foster."

Michael shakes his head and says, "I feel like a jerk."

"Come on, Michael. Be positive."

Sitting is the most normal position for a dog. The trick is to get him to do it on command. That requires know-how, time spent teaching the dog what to do, and then practicing with the dog. It is useful if you understand what's good about this command and why you should want your dog to learn it. Your dog's desire to sit occurs pretty often because he gets curious and wants to see what's going on. This command is the best techniques to gain control of the dog when he gets excited or distracted at an inconvenient time. Some dogs bark and get frantic when the doorbell rings or if someone walks by. You can control the dog once you get him into an obedience mode with a command that he's been taught. His sudden burst of energy could scare your caller half to death. If the dog has been taught the command *Sit,* you can control his frantic behavior by making him go into a *Sit* position. Of course, to do that properly, you must first command him to stop his wild behavior and then place him in the *Sit* position. That means you must first say *No,* and follow it up with *Sit* immediately afterward. If your dog were to get loose while on the street, it would be a lifesaver to be able to trigger the mechanism in his brain that makes him respond to *No, Sit, Stay,* all on your command. A properly trained dog will obey your commands unless his adrenaline is pumping like crazy from something like a dogfight or if he were running at top speed.

Okay. Here's something that applies to all the training sessions from now on: Do not feed your dog just before a training session. It will make him too sluggish to learn and may even stop the session because he will need to relieve himself. You are going to require all your dog's energy and his entire attention span whenever you teach him obedience commands. If his stomach is full, he will not be able to learn. Before you begin any teaching session, encourage your dog to relieve himself.

How to Teach Your Dog the Command *Sit*

To teach this or any other training command, I recommend the six-foot leather leash and metal training collar, which is also called the choke collar (see p. 100). These give you control of the dog and help you to keep his attention focused on you. Without these tools, you cannot train him.

When you begin your training program, it's a good idea to start out in a quiet place with no distractions because you don't know how the dog is going to respond. Try to make it as easy as possible by taking him to a quiet, out-of-the-way place in your neighborhood or to a secluded room indoors. I suggest that no one except family members should be allowed to watch, at least not in the beginning. If you've never done it before, training a dog for the first time in front of people can be an inhibiting experience. It's also distracting for the dog. You don't want friends, neighbors, or passersby for an audience. Only those who are actually involved with the training should be present. Always encourage the dog to relieve himself before beginning each session or he will not be able to concentrate.

Before beginning the session, bear in mind that *Sit* is not a command that allows you to use your dog's name when you say the command. You may only use the dog's name before giving him a command that involves moving forward. There are two commands in this course that involve forward movement: *Heel* and *Come When Called.*

Let me also remind you about the proper use of the leash and collar, because they are really important (see p. 99). Start out by placing the choke or training collar around the dog's neck properly. When it forms the letter *P*, it is on correctly. *P* is for perfect. When it forms the number 9, it is on wrong. Start out by attaching the leash to the collar. Next, open your right hand wide and hang the sewn loop, which is at the top of the leash onto your thumb. Take the middle of the leash with your left hand, create a loop, and drape it too over your right thumb so you have three leather straps of the leash in your right palm. Close your fingers tightly around the straps. With your right arm hanging straight down, the leash goes across your body diagonally to the dog's collar. Only two or three feet of the leash should be hanging across the front of your knees from your right hand to the dog's collar. Adjust the length of the leash from the collar to your right hand if necessary. It is easier to maintain control of the dog with a shorter length of leash. Holding the leash in this manner prevents your dog from yanking it out of your hand by surprise.

There are four different approaches to teaching *Sit,* and it's up to you to decide which one is the best for you and your dog. The first one is the Pushing Technique, which is the standard way to teach most dogs this command. The second one is the Placing Technique, which is for dogs that are sensitive in the lower area of their bodies and cannot tolerate pressure there. The third is the Food Technique, which is best for dogs that are extremely difficult to train because they are stubborn or very aggressive. The fourth is the Small-Dog Technique, which is meant to overcome the anxiety created in small dogs by humans who tower over them. I will describe each technique, and it is up to you to decide which one to use.

1. The Pushing Technique

This is the one I want to use for Foster, our little corgi friend. The proper use of the leash as you touch the dog is of primary importance with the Pushing Technique. The control exercised over the dog with the help of the leash is as much a part of the teaching process as the use of your hand, which pushes the dog in place.

"Lilly, bring Foster over here and watch what I do, please."

Lilly walks the dog over to Matty and hands him the leash.

"Thanks. Now, stand next to Foster, on his right side, so you both face in the same direction. With the leash in your right hand, gather it up so there is only twelve inches or less held over his head, and do not leave any slack."

"Like this, Matthew?"

"Yes. Now what I want you to do is locate the dog's little hip sockets with the fingers of your left hand. They're located at the base of his spine, one on each side. Run the

The Pushing
Technique

Stand or kneel at your dog's right side. With your left hand, grasp
his hip joints or hip sockets, which are at the base of his spine.
When you feel two indentations, press them firmly but gently with
your fingers. Say **Sit** as your left hand pushes down on the dog
and your right hand pulls up on the leash.

Photos by Jonathan Alcorn/Zuma.

fingers of your left hand from Foster's shoulder blades down the spine until you come to the end. Right there. Do you feel the indentation on each side?"

She smiles and pulls her hand away for a second.

"Ooh. That's a little weird."

"Come on, Mom. It's a lot nicer than changing diapers, isn't it?"

She smiles and puts her hand back on the little dog's spine.

"How do you know these things?" she asks, shaking her head.

"Hey, I'm Uncle Matty. Now, assuming you can feel both indentations with one hand at the same time, grab them with your fingers and gently squeeze them in a steady but firm manner. In a firm but friendly voice say, *Sit.*"

"Okay. Foster, sit."

"Yikes. Don't say the dog's name when giving this command. If you do, he will move forward. There. You see. Okay, Foster."

He takes the leash and swiftly walks the dog a few feet and hurrys back to Lilly, placing the leash in her hand.

"Oh, my little Foster. Matty's proud! Yes, you're a good boy."

The dog looks up at him. If Foster had a tail, he certainly would be wagging it. Matthew then whispers the rest of the instructions to the lady of the house.

"Okay, Mom. Show the family what you can do. Squeeze the indentations with your left hand and apply downward pressure to his rear end so he must go into a sitting position. As you push with your left hand, pull the leash upward with your right hand until it is taut but not uncomfortable for Foster. That's right. You're doing it. The idea is to push his rear down and his front up all at the same time. Look at you. See folks. Mom can do it the first time out. It just takes a bit of coordination. Think it through before starting or practice this in pantomime without the dog.

"You have to learn to say the command properly. Stretch the sound of the word "sit" until the dog is actually sitting. It makes an elongated, "*S-i-i-i-i-t.*" Say the command gently and with authority while you push down on his hips slowly and pull up on the leash steadily. With the proper pushing and pulling, the dog has no choice but to learn to sit as he hears the command. When the dog reaches the proper sitting position, praise him with great enthusiasm. The praise is an important part of the process. Don't forget, this is his motivation for pleasing you.

"Let me hear you praise him, Mom."

"What a good dog," said Lilly.

"Darling Lilly. If that's the best you can for this dog, then I'm calling the breeder. Come on. Say it like it was for Ben and Sally."

She takes in a deep breath and doesn't look up.

"Matthew, I'm gonna get you for this."

"Okay. But first give Foster what he needs."

"That's a good boy. Oh, my Foster. What a fabulous dog you are. Mommy loves you!"

"Now you're cooking. Listen, that dog will do anything for you. What do you think everyone? Did she do well?"

"Way to go, Mom," says Sally.

Do not work this method too hard or too fast or you might frighten the dog, and if you frighten him, you can't predict what he will do. If he becomes too scared, he may jump, run, or just lie down in defeat. Either way, it will ruin the lesson, which for all intents and purposes will be over.

Do not pet or stroke the dog when you praise him. A puppy may nip your fingers. More mature dogs could interpret affectionate petting as the lesson has ended. Create a voice that exudes very happy excitement at how well the dog is doing. Relate to the dog as you would a baby taking its first steps, and you might want to try my Uncle Matty falsetto voice, if you don't feel silly doing it. Try it without anyone around. I do it all the time and I do it in public. I have no shame.

Repeat the Pushing Technique over and over again, maybe fifty times, until the dog executes the command properly every time. The dog must get used to obeying commands from everyone in the family. Eventually you should try saying the command without pushing his rear down or pulling his front up into a sitting position. Say *Sit,* and slowly pull up on the leash with your right hand. Don't forget to praise the dog to the sky each and every time. It will not take very long for him to learn this.

During this teaching procedure do not correct the dog. Correcting a dog for something he has not yet learned is pointless and counterproductive. Then give your dog a rest. Allow him to relieve himself, but do not play with him. The session is not yet over.

After a five-minute rest, repeat the teaching process again and again. You may now begin to correct the dog if he fails to obey the command. At this time you should not have to push the dog's rear end down with your hand as you say the command word. But I'll tell you the truth, I don't think you're going to have to correct Foster here. He seems to have it but you never know.

If you give the command and Foster does not obey, administer a leash correction firmly but not too hard. Praise him immediately following each correction. If he does not go into the proper position or seems confused, begin the teaching process again. Take another break before you start over and wait a short while. Definitely do not release the dog from the session. After the break, go back to the command and repeat the lesson again another forty or fifty times. When I teach this at my kennel, I can get eight to ten *Sits* in a minute. It doesn't really take up too much time. Each half of the session should last about fifteen or twenty minutes. Most dogs will learn the command in the first session. Even though I consider this to be the most important command, it is the easiest one to teach. If the dog doesn't get it in the first session, give him a second session, but wait at least four hours. Never give more than two training sessions a day.

It may be necessary to use leash corrections if the dog does not respond properly or refuses to obey your *Sit* commands after a few sessions. Place the dog close to you at your left side. Gather all but two or three feet of the leash. Say *Sit,* and gently jerk the leash with your right hand as you push the dog down by the hip joints with your left hand. The dog, of course, has no choice but to get into the proper position. Praise him enthusiastically. This is very important. Repeat this procedure; with your right hand jerk the leash to the right as a leash correction, say *Sit,* pull the dog up with the leash, lower his rear end with your left hand. As he sits, praise him. Keep repeating this action until he sits immediately after your command without being pushed into it. Don't give him time to consider the command once it is given and never say the command more than once without making him respond properly.

My life-long formula for dog training has always been command, correction, and praise. It goes for every command in this book. Once you teach a dog a specific command, use a leash correction each and every time he does not respond properly. Say *Sit*. Then jerk the leash to the right and firmly say *No!* The dog will sit because he has been reminded to do so. Do not forget the formula: command, correction, and praise. Of course, if your dog responds to your command, do not give him a leash correction, instead go right to the praise. If he ignores the command, give him a leash correction and then praise him. If you want your dog to be trained properly, you must praise him immediately after every correction or command. That way the dog knows he has pleased you and will work for your approval.

2. The Placing Technique

Now here's a method that teaches *Sit* without the need for downward pressure on the dog's rear end. I recommend it for dogs that are too sensitive to be held or touched at the lower end of their bodies. Sometimes a dog has been hit or injured on the rump and will not let anyone touch him there. This includes dogs that have been hit anywhere, dogs that are shy, and dogs that for any number of reasons cannot accept the Pushing Technique. The Pushing Technique applies pressure on the hindquarters, which forces the dog into a sitting position; the Placing Technique does not.

This technique is ideal for frightened dogs because you will not be standing over them but, rather, placing yourself at the dog's eye level. This method is also kinder for dogs that have arthritis or hip dysplasia. *If your dog is not friendly, or is extremely shy or aggressive enough to bite, don't use this technique.* Most training techniques are offered here for the average dog based on the assumption that your dog does not bite.

This technique utilizes all of the elements in the Pushing Technique, with these exceptions:

If you are training a large dog, it is best to stand next to him. Smaller dogs require that you bend over or kneel next to your student. It all depends on the size of your dog. Hold the leash above the dog's head with your right hand and place your left hand behind the dog's hind legs. This replaces the hand positions in the Pushing Technique, where the hand is supposed to be on the dog's hip joints. Be gentle and firm. Move your left hand to your dog's rear legs at the first joint beneath the rump, which is the equivalent of the human knee. These joints bend forward naturally when the dog sits. Allow your palm to face upward as though you were scooping water.

Say the command, *Sit,* and as you do, push the dog's rear legs forward at the joint with your left hand. The legs give the impression that they are collapsing in a forward direction. At the same time, pull the leash up with your right hand and keep it taut. The dog will automatically move into the proper *Sit* position. Stretch the sound of the command until the dog is actually sitting. It should be elongated into "*S-i-i-i-i-t.*" Say the command gently but with authority as you push the dog's hind legs forward and pull up on the leash in a slow but steady pace. Don't forget to praise the dog after each command. Repeat the process at least fifty time until he responds properly every time.

3. The Food Technique

The third *Sit* technique requires that you follow all of the instructions from the first technique, the Pushing Technique, with a few exceptions. Food or some edible doggie snack that your dog really loves should be used as a motivator. This technique offers an incentive for dogs that bite or dogs that threaten to bite. It is also for very frightened dogs that are afraid of anyone coming near them.

The procedure for holding the leash is the same as in the Pushing Technique. Place the food or doggie snack of choice in your left hand, show it to your hungry student, hold it close to his nose, and then brush it slowly past his eyes. Hold it about six inches above his head so he must look up at it. It should make him salivate and become restless with desire for the morsel. Once the dog focuses on the treat, say *Sit,* and slowly begin pulling the leash straight up, above his head. Keep the dog's focus on the food, which is also above his head, and keep it far enough away so he cannot get it. The pulling of the leash in an upward direction gets the dog into a Sit position because his full attention is probably on the food treat. Once he sits, praise him generously, and allow him to have the treat. Repetition is the key to dog training. Keep repeating the steps outlined until the dog responds properly. If you feel the dog now understands the command, try getting him to *Sit* without the food. Slowly pull up on the leash with your right hand as you give the command, *Sit.* Always praise the dog after he goes into the *Sit* position properly. Remember the formula, command, correction, praise. Do not use leash or verbal corrections until you are sure that the dog knows the command but is simply refusing to obey. That does happen.

4. The Small-Dog Technique

Humans often overwhelm very small dogs with their height, and the dogs understandably become frightened or intimidated during training. Many behavior problems never even get started when owners use the Small-Dog Technique because it does not instill in small dogs the fear of being trained. Use the same basic instructions as in the Pushing Technique, along with a few exceptions. Under no circumstance should you tower above your canine student. Try bending over, or kneeling next to the dog as you teach him this command. With a very, very small dog, place him on a table for his lessons. The table puts you both on a level playing field. When the height difference between the dog and the trainer is not so great, training becomes far less frightening for such dogs. You may then use the Pushing Technique or the Placing Technique for teaching the command *Sit* to a small dog.

Sit for Dogs of Different Temperaments

If your dog has a High-Energy temperament, maintain a positive attitude about him. Concentrate on the outgoing aspect and how great that is. When teaching *Sit,* stay close to the dog and work in a confined space that is quiet with no distractions or audience. Use a firm and authoritative tone of voice. It should communicate that this is not playtime and now is the time for learning. Leash corrections depend on the dog's size; age; breed; and tolerance. A toy breed needs to be handled much more gently than sporting breeds, working breeds, hounds, and so on. A quick jerk and release is the best way to administer a leash correction for High-Energy dogs.

If your dog has a Shy temperament, put yourself in his place. Teaching sessions for *Sit* could jangle your nerves. Being frightened most of the time is not the ideal condition for learning something new and strange. You must be patient and considerate. Body language is very important when training a Shy dog. Do not stand over a Shy dog, especially if he is a small animal. Kneel down next to him whenever you are going to relate to him. A very small dog should be taught this command on a table, so he sees you at eye level. Use a reassuring tone of voice and be certain the dog knows you love him and approve of him. My Uncle Matty falsetto voice is very effective for Shy dogs. Try it. A Shy dog is like a shy child and they both should be treated in a similar manner. Leash corrections should be gentle or not given at all. Hold the leash very loosely and try to hold the dog in place with gentle pressure. Actually, the Placing Technique is best for teaching *Sit* to shy dogs. Teach this command in a quiet place with no distractions. The only people present at the session should be you and members of your family. Teach the dog next to a barrier or wall. This has a calming effect.

If your dog has a Strong-Willed temperament and is stubborn, you must be patient and understanding. Do not think of him as a bad dog. Be persistent and you will eventually teach this kind of dog whatever he needs to learn. Exercise him before each lesson. Use the Placing Technique and kneel down next to the dog during the teaching process for the best results. If you must stand because of the dog's size, use the Pushing Technique but work quickly before the dog has a chance to think about it and decides not to cooperate. Use a firm tone of voice but do not be harsh. Yelling or vocal intimidation is not going to be effective. Use firm leash corrections but do not be excessive or abusive. Increase the intensity of each correction if the dog absolutely refuses to respond. Start out using gentle leash corrections and increase the pressure as necessary. Sometimes a fast jerk works best and sometimes just pulling up slowly and forcing the dog to sit works. It's a matter of doing what works. Teach *Sit* to a Strong-Willed dog in a quiet place where there are no distractions or spectators.

If your dog has an Easygoing or Sedate temperament, accept him the way he is because he is never going to be different. You must tolerate his slower rhythm. That is who he is. If the dog is small, kneel next to him when teaching this command. Stand next to him if he is large. Be affectionate, positive, enthusiastic, and uninhibited in giving him hugs, kisses, and lots of praise. If the dog lies down in the middle of the lesson, pick him up and try to recharge his battery with your enthusiasm. Use a very happy, energized tone of voice. You must be enthusiastic with this type of dog. Motivate him with funny sounds, whistling, and puppy talk. Yes, I said puppy talk. When you first begin to administer leash corrections, jerk the leash in a soft manner. Gradually increase the intensity to a medium degree if it becomes necessary. Once the dog is used to leash corrections and accepts them without resentment, use a firm, normal leash correction. Do not correct the dog if he does not understand the command. But you must correct him if he is aloof or is not willing to obey. Train him in any place where you are both comfortable but that is noise-free and without distractions. Do not allow anyone else to be present unless they are members of the family.

If your dog has an Aggressive temperament, you must

always be aware of the fact that your dog may growl, snap, or even bite when you try to teach him this command. Be careful about getting bitten when teaching this command. This is especially the case for a dog that has bitten someone before. You must never stand over an Aggressive dog or make direct eye contact. Such gestures can be threatening or challenging to a dog. Be aware of how your dog responds to being touched by you or anyone else before beginning the teaching process. If the dog was ever hit, he may have an aggressive response to being handled or touched. Be cautious and move slowly. The dog's behavior can be changed by stroking him gently and lovingly, and by speaking in a loving tone of voice at the same time. Do this all the time, whether you are training the dog or not.

Dominant-Aggressive and Fear-Aggressive dogs require different tones of voice. Young Dominant-Aggressive dogs require a stern but not harsh tone. As they begin to mature, your tone of voice should be more authoritative and demanding. A professional trainer should handle mature dogs of this temperament. Young Fear-Aggressive dogs need a gentle tone of voice but one that is firm enough to get the point across. As they mature, you can use a firmer but not harsh vocal tone. A professional dog trainer should train fully grown Fear-Aggressive dogs. The dog's age, size, and intensity of aggression must determine how you employ leash corrections. Young dogs between seven weeks and six months should be corrected with short, snappy leash jerks that are not too hard. Between six and ten months, use quick, firm jerks. Dogs of that age may require harder jerks, depending on just how aggressive they are. Such dogs must be corrected the instant they behave aggressively. These techniques must be done until the aggressive behavior stops. These techniques will work most of the time, unless the dog is so aggressive that only a professional dog trainer can handle him. Train Aggressive dogs in your home or some other private area. No distractions should be allowed to interfere with the training and that means spectators including children, neighbors, or other members of the family. Once the dog becomes fully mature, it is too dangerous for anyone other than a professional to train such dogs. It is important to have your adult, Aggressive dog evaluated by a dog trainer or animal behaviorist.

"Okay, Bennett family. Do we now know what to do with Foster?"

They all agree.

"Okay, Foster, come to me. Oh, Mr. F. What a good job you did. Matty's proud."

Five
Walk This Way

Heel and the Automatic Sit

When I was a kid, I used to try to get the end piece of the rye bread before anyone else. We called it the battle for the heel. Well, years later in dog training the battle for the *Heel* was very different. No, I'm not talking about the heel of the bread or the heel of your shoe. I'm talking about teaching your dog to walk nicely with you on the street or down the road without pulling your arm or dragging you along. Of course, I'm talking about a dog walking in *Heel*. I'm talking about a leash and a collar with a dog at one end and a person at the other. A well-*Heel*ed dog is not one that's flush with money. It is a dog that walks in *Heel*, that stays with his owner when they're out walking and trots along at the same pace.

When your dog *Heels*, he walks with you without pulling on the leash. When you walk, he walks. When you stop, he stops and then sits, no matter what distractions there are and no matter where you go. A dog that has been trained to walk in *Heel* will do this in the city, in the country, with or without distractions, and keep his mind on you. If he does it properly, he walks on your left side with his head next to your leg. A well-trained dog never leaves your side once he's been given the command *Heel.* I'll discuss the Automatic Sit later in the chapter.

If you can't get your dog to walk alongside you without pulling, then you cannot really walk your dog properly, and that's a shame. It's also a safety issue because a strong dog can pull hard at the leash, break it, or force it out of your hands if you're not paying strict attention, and then possibly run out into street traffic. Don't get mad at me. I'm just the messenger with the bad news. But, I also have good news: Teaching your dog to walk in *Heel* sounds harder than it seems. If you do teach your dog this command, you will enjoy your dog in safety and comfort. Think about it and ask yourself if walking your dog is a pleasant experience. Taking walks with your dog should be one of life's really great pleasures. At least it's supposed to be. You go out in all sorts of weather and take a healthy, pleasant walk and meet your friends and neighbors, some of them with their dogs. What could be better? *Heel* is one command that is not only useful, it is necessary. Getting your dog to do it properly is not a trick and it's not hard to teach. But the command forces the dog to go against his desires and natural curiosity but not against his natural instincts. In the winter, a wolf pack will tread slowly in a single file through the snow, moving from one part of their range to another searching for food. To teach your dog to *Heel* requires some patience, determination, and a lot of repetition.

And speaking of *Heel,* I am at this moment in New York

146 The Ultimate Guide to Dog Training

City and about to teach an unruly dog the fine art of walking down the streets of Manhattan. I'm at 63rd Street and Broadway, in the heart of Lincoln Center, and I'm close to all the glamorous concert halls and opera houses. I am surrounded by the many tall apartment houses that frame Lincoln Center, and they all seem to have a lot of dogs living inside. Many of these dogs are out on the busy streets, behaving themselves as they take their owners for a nice gentle walk. Isn't it nice that they let people live in these buildings, too? There are a lot of dogs in Manhattan. It must be because there is no curfew. Hey, don't blame me for that one. Complain to Siegal.

The reason I'm here is because Larry Groenig and Phil Waterman sent up the bat signal for me. I go where the problems are because I am Uncle Matty, a dog's best friend. Larry and Phil have a thirteen-month-old Labrador Retriever named Brownie, and they share everything connected with the dog, including feeding him; exercising him, which is a major deal with a Lab; cleaning up after him, another big deal in the city; and walking him. Walking the dog is the problem. How would you like to be dragged down Broadway by a ninety-pound roller coaster with hair? The dog doesn't stop for lights, either. Instead, traffic steps aside for Brownie. I've even seen bike messengers pull over for this dog and check their pulse rate. With a dog like this you don't need legs, you need *wheels.* You don't get to walk much with a dog like Brownie; you do the slide-step half-run, which is dangerous and tricky because you can't stop yourself from stepping in whatever is lying in front of you, if you get my drift. Brownie is a sweet dog but he knocks over everyone in his path because of his exuberance.

"Hey, Larry. Say hello."

"Hello."

"Come on, Larry. Talk to me."

"What do you want me to say?"

"Excuse me. I guess Larry is shy. He is about five feet, seven inches tall, a nice-looking guy."

"Oh, boy. I guess I better do the talking if that's all you can talk about. I'm a dog person. I have always been a dog person. I love them. I grew up with dogs and have no problem with them. As a matter of fact, at one time I wanted to be a vet or at least be in the dog business."

"And now you're in advertising, right?"

"Right."

"Now your friend, Phil, who is six feet two inches, two hundred and twenty pounds, a really big guy, is not a dog person. He has never had a dog. Is he scared of them, Larry? Come on. You can tell Uncle Matty."

"Excuse me?"

"Oh, is that you, Phil? I didn't think you were going to say anything."

"Uncle Matty, I appreciate you coming here to help us with the Beast That Ate Broadway, but I was having my breakfast," said Phil.

"What're you having and would you give your old Uncle Matty a bite?"

"Sure. It's a typical New York street breakfast. Coffee to go, a bagel with cream cheese, and a prune Danish."

Larry laughs.

"Well, that's good for the arteries, isn't it? But seriously. Did I really say 'but seriously'? Anyway, you are absolutely right, Uncle Matty. Phil is scared of dogs and that's all there is to that."

Matty shakes his finger at Larry.

"So if you think Phil is scared of them, why did you get a dog?"

"Who knew? Who would have thought someone that huge would be scared of anything? I have always loved dogs, and I thought everyone else did, too. I've been rooming with this guy for five years and I had no idea about him and the dog thing."

"What do you mean?"

"Matty, how should I put it? The dog walks into the living room and Phil's knuckles turn white, his eyes turn to satellite dishes glowing in the dark, and suddenly he sounds like he's speaking Bulgarian. Hello! What's wrong with this picture? Big guy, scared of dog."

"Tell me, Phil, what do you do for a living?"

Phil mumbles something.

"I'm sorry, I didn't hear that."

"I'm a bouncer in a bar."

"Yikes."

Phil shakes his head and says, "I swear, Uncle Matty, I am not scared of dogs. But you know what? I am scared to walk Brownie."

Larry says, "See? What'd I say? He's afraid of the dog."

Phil answers, "That's not a dog. That's a hurricane with a tongue."

"Hold it, guys. Time out. Let me tell you something. If we can teach that furry cyclone to walk nicely, to walk gently, to walk in *Heel,* I'll bet all this bickering will stop."

"For how much?" says Larry.

"Never mind. Just listen to your old Uncle Matty."

Before we start, remember my rule for teaching every command. Avoid feeding your dog before any session.

Eating will make a dog drowsy, sluggish, and too content with things just the way they are. Training is a bit easier if you feed your dog after each session rather than before. No matter where you train your dog, indoors or out, encourage him to relieve himself before starting a lesson. If you don't, you may have to interrupt the lesson in the middle to let him go because he will not be able to concentrate on what you're teaching him. Pick a quiet place to train your dog, one that has as few distractions as possible. *Heel* is a command that is really best taught outdoors because you need the space to walk around in. Do not allow an audience to gather. You, and maybe other members of the household who are going to be walking the dog in the future, have to be alone with the dog.

The first time a young puppy hits the street he is either going to be scared out of his mind and hug the wall of the closest building, or he is going to want to go everywhere and do everything, usually all at once. The great outdoors, even your neighborhood, is an adventure for a puppy or a dog heading out for the first time. It's all new and exciting, with intriguing sights, sounds, smells, people, and other dogs, especially other dogs. Actually the same is true for any dog that is cooped up in the house all night or day and is taken outside to relieve himself and get a bit of exercise. This certainly applies to Brownie, the Loch Ness Labrador. His breed is an exuberant one. Labs love everything and everybody and get very excited the minute they hit the bricks. They need people, they need exercise, and they need several walks a day if they live in the city.

Daily walks are as important to dogs as their food. Once they are outside, they forget about everything you've done for them and will run wild if you let them. They want to see it all and see it as fast as they can. That's why your arm gets sore from walking them. That's why it's important to train your dog how to walk properly with you, and to teach him that *you* are what he must focus on when out for a walk or a training session. The dog's first response to the outside will be to run ahead, straining at the leash as he pulls you down the street. You must teach him the command *Heel.*

Whether your dog is trained or not, going outside is the high point of his day and always will be. Even though you're going to curb his desire to run, jump, and frolic at your expense by teaching him *Heel,* you don't want him to dread each session. You must not allow the training session to become a battle. Keep the training sessions upbeat by showing the dog some enthusiasm as you walk to and from the training area. Try to keep him in a happy mood.

As in all training commands, communication is how you get the dog to do the things he has to do. Dog training provides the communication with the leash, verbal commands, use of *No* and *Okay,* and the tone of your voice. Dogs respond to our tone of voice, which can convey happiness, sadness, enthusiasm, and many variations of those attitudes. They also respond to how loud or soft you speak, and to the inflection of your voice. When you say to a dog "I love you" in a happy, high-pitched tone of voice, he will stop what he's doing and come right up to you for more. The reverse is true if you shout "No" in a harsh tone.

You can always get your dog's attention without a leash correction or verbal reprimand by raising your voice several octaves and speaking to him as you would to a baby: "What a dog! Are you the good dog? Good boy!" This is especially true if you speak in a high-pitch tone and with enthusiasm and praise. If you use the right tone of voice, your dog will listen to you. Add training to the equation and the dog will do anything you train him to do.

How to Teach Your Dog the Command *Heel*

Give your dog two sessions a day and try to keep them down to fifteen minutes each. Conduct them several hours apart.

"Okay, Larry, let's do something with Brownie. Let me have his leash."

Larry and Phil hand the leash along with Brownie over to Matty.

"Thank you. I have him now. Hey, good boy. How's my beautiful Brownie. Yeah, oh my. You're the dog in the show, aren't you?"

The large dog's tail moves swiftly. Brownie becomes so excited that he appears to be moving in three, maybe four, separate sections, like a huge plastic toy. Matty starts to run down the street with him and then stops. Brownie keeps his eyes on Matty.

"Hey, that was good. You did me proud. Did I say proud? Yes, I did. Uncle Matty's soooo proud!"

Teaching *Heel* begins with putting your dog in the proper position. The correct position for *Heel* is to place your dog on your left side, next to your knee. Later on it becomes important to maintain the proper position, but in the beginning the dog can be off a little. In the early lessons, the dog will have done all right if he only stays two or three feet ahead. But by the third lesson, he must be corrected whenever he strays from your left knee. The tradition of placing the dog on the left side began with hunters working with dogs. They carried their weapons with their right arm and the dog walked next to them on the left.

You must have a six-foot leather leash and metal training collar for all these commands. Place both hands on the leash in the correct position for the leash correction. Let your arms dangle loose and straight. Allow three feet of the leash to drape across your knees (see p. 108). Keep your hands down near your waist. The leash should be held as though you were going to administer a leash correction. This is important for walking in *Heel.*

"Okay, now I have Brownie and I'm going to use his name for this command. It's an important part of the command. When you and the dog get into the proper position to start out in *Heel,* say, "Brownie, *Heel!* Come on, boy. Yes, you're doing great. What a good dog."

Matty and the dog begin to walk forward along Broadway. Because of the traffic, Matty raises his voice to be heard. Larry and Phil watch and are surprised that Brownie is not quite as frantic as he is with them.

"Hey, what's the trick? Why isn't he running down the street like a fire engine?" asked Phil.

"Hey, I'm Uncle Matty. This dog wouldn't dare yank me. Now, pay attention. You must always use your dog's name for this command . . ."

Suddenly, Matty is caught by surprise as Brownie decides to run for New Jersey and practically pulls him out into the street. Matty stops suddenly and turns around, walks in the opposite direction.

He yells, "Brownie, *Heel,*" in a booming voice, catching the big Lab by surprise and then walks in the opposite direction.

The dog is almost knocked off his feet as he meets the force of an
unforgiving leash going south. Matty pushes his hair back with
his hand and continues as if nothing happened.

Heel is an action command, and the use of Brownie's
name makes him aware that he is about to move in a forward direction. By saying his name before the actual command, you get the dog's attention. When you say his
name, his focus should be on you. He can't help it. Most
of us would look up at someone saying our name. Hearing
his name makes him ready to move. On the command
"Brownie, *Heel,*" start walking, stepping off with your left
foot. We always step off with the left foot because the dog
sees it first, and when it moves, he moves. Stepping off
with the left foot gets you and the dog moving together at
the same time. The idea is to encourage the dog to walk by
your side. There are a number of predictable mistakes the
dog may make when you start this command the way I described it. I'm going to list each one and discuss how to
deal with it. The first mistake is common to every dog.
They're going to do what Brownie just did to me.

He's Going to Run Ahead.

Once you step off, you know the dog is going to be so
excited that he springs forward and gets as far ahead of
you as the leash will allow. He will probably pull hard and
try to drag you with him, like the Brown behemoth just
did. But, because you are on top of the situation, you will
know what to do: Allow the dog to run as far and as fast as
he wants, until he reaches the end of his rope, which is the
six-foot training leash. When he reaches the end of it,
make a sharp, hard turn to the right, immediately followed by another right turn. That means you will have

Stand at your dog's right side with one-third to one-half of the leash gathered in your hands. Keep your hands waist-high. Say your dog's name, followed by the verbal command **Heel.**

Step forward with your left foot, which is closest to the dog and get him moving as you move.

Photos by Jonathan Alcorn/Zuma.

made a U-turn and will be walking in the opposite direction. There will be a moment of physical conflict when the dog wants to go one way but the force of your turn and the strength of the leash will not permit this. At the moment that you turn say, "Brownie, *Heel*" in a loud, authoritative voice. Praise him immediately. Then hurry in the opposite direction without losing any momentum. It is important for the dog to be completely surprised and turned in the direction you are walking without having any choice in the matter. Encourage him to catch up with you by constantly praising him and patting your thigh as a sort of giddiyup. You are demonstrating to your dog that you are the leader of his pack. His instincts will come into play and, if he is typical of most dogs, he will not only accept this, he will have new respect for you. This is a major step toward getting your dog obedience-trained.

"Okay, which one of you guys wants to try this?"

Silence.

"Phil, why don't you give it a shot?"

Phil stammers out his reply, "Ah, I don't think this is a good idea, Matty."

"Oh, sure it is. You have to start handling the dog sometime. It might as well be now. Besides, do you want Larry to confirm that you are really afraid of dogs?"

Phil takes the leash from Matty's hands and, surprisingly, holds it in the proper position.

"That's good. All right, Phil. Okay, you've got the dog standing at your left side. Do you remember what to do?"

"I think so."

Phil holds the leash with both hands. He looks straight ahead and concentrates so hard you can hear his brain clicking.

"Brownie, *Heel!*"

"Very good, Phil. Great start. You're doing great."

Phil steps off with his left foot and starts to move forward. Brownie does not move and holds his ground like a statue. Phil does not realize that Brownie has not budged and is jerked hard as he reaches the end of the leash. Caught by surprise, the leash slides out of Phil's hand and he trips over it.

Larry says, "Well that's cute. I thought the dog was supposed to get tripped up. You handled the leash like a cargo net."

Matty intercedes.

"Will you please leave him alone. He's going to be fine. You'll see. Are you sure you two are friends? Okay, Phil, at least you know what to do."

Matty puts his arm around Phil and speaks to him very quietly, so Larry can't hear him.

"But Phil, baby, pay attention to the dog. You have to keep an eye on him, just as he has to keep one on you. This is all about the dog. Watch the dog and you can't go wrong."

Phil nods and hands the leash back to Matty.

"Other than that you were perfect. You'll get it. Once you and the dog are moving forward, you keep making turns.

"Maintain your pace, do not stop walking, and allow the dog to catch up with you. Once he has positioned himself next to your left leg, slide the leash to the original length you started with. Just repeat the whole thing if the dog starts to run ahead again. Turn right quickly, say, 'Brownie, *Heel.* Good boy!' then turn right again, making a complete U-turn. Each time you turn say 'Brownie, *Heel.* Good boy!' Then keep walking at a steady clip in the opposite direction. It's going to be hard on the dog each time you turn in the opposite direction. To compensate for the strain on the dog, praise him generously after each time you say the command. Praise him even more lavishly when he catches up to you. I'm telling you that the praise will get him to want to keep up with you and learn what the command *Heel* is really about. Praise is an important part of the communication with your dog. When you praise him for something he just did, he understands that what he did was a good thing. It tells him he is good if he walks by your side. The praise also encourages him to stay focused on you so he won't be caught off guard when you make more turns or stops. Some dogs need to be praised immediately after the surprise turn for encouragement while it is best to pause a second or two before offering the praise to high energy or overly exuberant dogs. Some dogs crave the reassurance instantly while others interpret the praise as a signal that work is over for the day. This varies from dog to dog, based on temperament. If you maintain an awareness of this factor, it won't take long to figure out how and when to praise your dog."

He May Lag Behind.

Running ahead is not the only problem when teaching *Heel*. Sometimes you will find the dog lags behind you. If you keep praising the dog and giving him lots of verbal encouragement, this problem is going to get fixed quickly. Tell him what a good dog he is and say anything you can to coax him to catch up. Keep inviting him to walk by your side so he maintains focus on you and tries to catch up. In some cases, the dog will not respond properly to your summons. If that becomes a problem, gently jerk the leash or pull it as you continue to praise and encourage the dog.

Try to get the dog to develop the habit of keeping his attention fixed on you every time he is taken outside for a walk.

Sharpening His Walk.

After the dog has had three or four lessons, it is time to sharpen his ability to find and hold the exact position he should be in when walking in *Heel.* No one could expect the dog, by himself, to find the exact place his head should be when walking with you. If he's been keeping one or two lengths ahead or behind, that's fine. However, it is now time to learn the exact place for him to line up with you. He must learn to align his head with your left leg and hold that position. He must be neither farther ahead nor behind your left leg.

Place the dog in the *Sit* position, as you did for the first lesson. Say "Brownie, *Heel.*" Take the first step with your left foot and start walking. The goal is to teach the dog to keep his head aligned with your leg. Whenever he pulls ahead, lags behind, or moves away from your leg, give him a leash correction and say *No* in a firm tone of voice. Make a right turn quickly and say, "Good boy." Then make a complete U-turn. On each turn say, "Brownie, *Heel.* Good Boy." Continue to walk in the opposite direction. Always praise the dog after each correction or verbal command. Repeat this procedure again and again until you're convinced he knows what you expect him to do when walking in *Heel.* Your dog may sharpen and maintain his position in a single fifteen-minute session. If not, repeat the technique for as long as it takes him to learn it. Fifteen-minute sessions are about the limit for any dog before he tires out. Give him four hours rest between lessons. Two lessons a day are best.

Walking a Shy Dog.

Some dogs are shy and have a hard time being outside. A new home or a new outdoor environment are difficult situations for them. Shy dogs are frightened of the outdoor hubbub and activity. They may be too frightened to even walk once outside the first time. This is often the situation with puppies. The shy dog and the shy puppy cringe with panic and either hide under your legs or hug the nearest wall. If the dog is terrified of being outside, you must help him calm down and adjust. Do not be too dominant or you will never get him past his fright. Teaching *Heel* is the ideal way to help a shy dog adjust to being outside. The command will distract him from his fear. He is now forced to focus on you.

Place a leash and collar on him but do not expect him to be an easy student. He will probably refuse to walk at first. If that happens, move in front of him and kneel down to his height. Be sweet and gentle and try to entice him with playful sounds and gestures. Do anything that calms him down, gets his attention, makes him feel good. Your tone of voice is important. Be friendly and outgoing. Get him to come to you. When he comes to you, give him lots of praise and pats and take hold of his leash while you do this so he does not notice it. Keep repeating this action until the dog feels secure enough to come to you each time you bend down. Once he does that, back away each time he walks to you and try doing it as you hold the leash. When you lengthen the distance each time the dog comes to you, you are forcing him to adjust to walking with you in an outdoor setting, and he will not even realize it.

At some point (and you will know when) as you call the dog to you from a kneeling position, it will seem natural to stand up, take hold of the leash in the proper way, and start walking together in the same direction. A stubborn dog may refuse to walk at this point. If that's the case, keep walking, pulling him along until he gives in. Try not to scrape his paws too hard along the sidewalk. The pads under his feet are delicate and can be injured easily from too much friction. This will create a pain that he won't forget and that will only add to his fear of walking outdoors. Take him to a grassy area if he continues to struggle. At least the grass will prevent him from scraping his paws if he refuses to walk and you need to pull him.

Negotiating a New Leash.

Wearing a leash for the first time is not easy for many dogs, especially puppies. Some simply don't know what a leash is and fear it. Others sense the minute they have it on that they have lost control and resist it vigorously. It is very possible that you cannot begin to teach the command *Heel* until you deal with the problem of leash rejection.

Dogs who refuse to adjust to a leash will bite at it, push and pull it with their paws, and do a sort of twisting dance in a futile effort to get it off. They simply do not want to be controlled. However, because you are responsible for your dog's safety and well-being, you must understand that a leash is not only a dog training tool. It is a daily lifesaver because it restrains a dog from his own impulses and prevents him from running into traffic. And, of course, it is also an extremely important way to communicate with your dog. You must not accept your dog's refusal to wear a leash.

You cannot train a dog without a leash. Some dogs accept the leash immediately, while others resist it because they are frightened or not used to it. Do not wait to apply a leash to your new dog. To get him to accept a leash without too much fuss, use a buckled collar and attach a lightweight leash to it. You can even use a clothesline if you like. Allow the dog to drag the leash around all day so he becomes used to it. The idea is to accustom the dog to the feel and the weight of the leash and collar. Be certain the collar fits well and is comfortable. To avoid accidents, never leave the dog alone with the leash attached to him. After several days of dragging the leash around, the dog should get used to the idea of it. Always be cheerful and upbeat when attaching the leash to his collar.

Pick up the leash many times a day when the dog is dragging it around. Be relaxed as you do it and apply no tension to the line, as you would if you were taking him out for a walk. Until the dog is ready to be taught the *Heel* command, allow him to pull you and take care not to use the leash in a negative manner.

After each verbal correction, praise the dog generously. Leash resistance may be expressed three ways: by the paws, the mouth, or the teeth. If a dog paws the leash or bites it, say *No* firmly and pull the leash away. Do not forget to praise your dog after the verbal correction.

If your dog wears the leash much of the time for several days, he will adjust to it. When he does, you can discard the lightweight leash and switch to a conventional six-foot, five-eighths-of-an-inch-wide leather leash. Once he seems to have made an adjustment to the leash in the house, try walking outdoors. As I said before, begin on a soft, grassy surface. If he resists walking on-leash, the grass will prevent his paws from painfully scraping against the sidewalk. If your dog refuses to walk while on-leash, kneel and call him to you in a happy, loving tone of voice. When he finally comes to you, praise him lavishly. Try to create a pleasant association with the leash. If the dog rejects the leash no matter what you do, it may be necessary to consult a professional dog trainer.

Jumping While Teaching *Heel.*

You cannot allow your dog's exuberance while outdoors to prevent you from teaching him this command. An energetic, excitable dog is almost certain to continually jump on people on the street during his training session. Jumping is a happy, although unacceptable, gesture that is not only annoying to those that you meet but is also disruptive for the lesson. Use a leash correction each time he jumps on someone and say in a firm tone of voice, *No!* Once you start correcting your dog for jumping on people, you must consistently enforce the correction both indoors and outdoors.

Wrapping Himself Around Your Legs.

Some dogs will cling to you for protection and quickly entangle your legs as you try to walk with them. These are dogs that are overly affectionate and greatly devoted. Insecurity, shyness, acute sensitivity, or extreme affection may cause this. Whatever the reason, the situation is ridiculous and an impossibility for taking your dog on a walk.

This is the only time in training where I want you to use your left hand to hold the leash while walking in *Heel.* If your dog tends to wrap himself around your legs when you walk, then you should keep placing him in the correct stance while you step forward and keep encouraging him with praise and compliments. Keep his head aligned with your left leg. It is easier to keep him in the proper position if you hold the leash with your left hand and maneuver him back where he belongs when he starts to go in toward your legs. Hold him in place with your left hand as you walk, and give him fewer leash corrections than usual as you manipulate the dog with a soothing tone of voice. When you first start teaching this command to an overly affectionate dog, it is more important to stress the proper position than the other aspects of the command. Do not be too forceful with a nervous or frightened dog. Love and kindness are the only techniques that will rid him of his fear.

Walking in Toward You.

Last but not least is the problem of the dog turning in toward you as he begins walk in *Heel.* This causes you and the dog to fall over each other as you keep crossing paths. Making an excessive amount of right turns while teaching *Heel* may cause this particular form of behavior. Just give the dog a leash correction whenever he deviates from the straight and narrow path and use a variety of right and left turns during each training session. At the same time you give the leash correction firmly say *No!* Then make a left or right turn, depending on how far inward he has strayed. As you turn, your knee will gently force him to turn with you. Don't forget to praise him. Then say, "Brownie, *Heel.*" Continue walking. Praise him again. Follow this pattern every time he walks into you.

Heel for Dogs of Different Temperaments

If your dog has a High-Energy temperament, teach him to walk alongside you in a calm, obedient manner. You know he's going to pull ahead, veer to each side, pause, start again, and scurry in reverse. You may find yourself caught in a struggle. The dog has no interest in which way he walks and in what direction. This is of concern only to the person walking him. If he was walking alone, he would not adhere to a straight line or stay on the left or right side of anything. It's not his nature to align himself with your leg. There is a tendency to pull on the leash so hard during the teaching of this command that the collar really does choke him in an effort to get him to obey you and walk the right way. You must be patient with a dog of this temperament and try to be cool and calm.

It's a good idea to vary your moves, which will prevent you from allowing the dog to figure out where you're going to turn or what you're going to do before you do it. Keep him guessing. If you are not predictable, the dog will have to focus on you, and when he stays focused on you, he will learn faster.

When you teach this command, and when you are practicing, stay in a good mood. Use a calm and restrained tone of voice when the dog needs to be corrected. When you use your voice in the leash corrections, be determined, consistent, and authoritative. Your leash corrections should be medium to firm. That's a judgment call on your part. Only you can tell what your High-Energy dog needs from moment to moment.

Where you teach your dog this command is important. It should be outdoors, but it is important that you remain in a private situation. Your own yard is best, if you have one. You may have to teach the dog outdoors away from your home, but the place you choose must be quiet and secluded. No distractions should interfere with your dog's ability to learn. If you gather an audience, it will distract both you and the dog and slow down or eliminate the learning process.

If your dog has a Shy temperament, he may have a hard time walking with you. It is not out of the question that he will need to adjust to wearing a leash. You're going to be stretched to the limit when you try to teach a Shy dog to *Heel*, and it's going to be hard to keep yourself from getting frustrated. Your Shy dog may also be too frightened to do anything outdoors that you need him to do. A Shy dog may stay close to your leg; he may even hug it. You must remain unruffled, smooth, efficient, but considerate. If you understand that the dog is trying to cope with his fear, it will help you be more understanding and patient. If you have a second dog, or if your neighbor has one, your Shy dog may follow him around during the teaching of *Heel*. A second dog could be used the same way for leash-breaking, too. You must maintain a cool, even frame of mind if you're going to get your Shy dog trained. Do not pull or choke him with the leash. Allow him to drag it around. Shy dogs sometimes react to a leash the same way some horses object to getting the bit in their mouths the first time.

When first teaching *Heel* to a Shy dog, you may find that he is too frightened to walk with you because your large body makes him feel threatened. The way to handle this is to first face the dog and then get close to the ground. The idea is to avoid posing any threat to your dog. Kneel next to him for a while or lie down and face him. Your tone of voice should be soft, loving, and reassuring. Do not use any verbal corrections for a Shy dog. Very gentle leash corrections are all you can use to communicate a negative message to a Shy dog. Maintain a light touch with your use of the leash, as if it were a single strand of pearls. Find a quiet, secluded location to teach this command. A Shy dog may resist the use of the leash, so you should avoid teaching the command on a cement sidewalk or an asphalt street or driveway. Those surfaces could injure your dog's feet if he resists the leash by pulling away from you. Find a grassy surface or carpet; not tile, linoleum, or any slippery surface. This command is hard enough for a Shy dog without making it harder.

If your dog has a Strong-Willed temperament, you should be ready for a struggle. A Strong-Willed dog may insist on going in every direction except the one you desire. He'll veer off to the left, to the right, run in front of you, and lag behind you. You must not forget that you are in charge. The best advice is for you to not lose your composure. Study the techniques for this command well, know them inside and out, and be prepared for your dog's resistance. Know what to do when the dog tries to go his own way. Stay in control no matter what the dog does.

Be consistent with your body language. Stand straight and do not give him the idea he can bully you. Make him keep up with you, continuing to walk in the same direction no matter what. Be unyielding and insist that the dog stay next to your left leg at all times. The dog may try running in every different direction, but you will win if you are as stubborn as the dog, and just keep walking in a consistently straight line.

Your tone of voice should be firm, clear, and authoritative. Voice corrections must be strict. Say each command and each verbal correction with a no-nonsense attitude. Never *ask* your dog to *Heel. Make* him do it. Each leash correction should be firm with the intensity depending on the size and the age of the dog. It is best, and in the long run kinder, to administer one really firm correction instead of many mild ones. Too many corrections won't help. What helps is your attitude and determination to stay in charge and get your way. A Strong-Willed dog needs to be taught *Heel* in a quiet, private place with no distractions.

If your dog has an Easygoing or Sedate temperament, then you should be somewhat calm and easygoing yourself. You must be encouraging and positive so you do not upset a dog of this kind. Be patient. When you praise the dog, you must praise him to the sky so he is impressed with how much you like what he's doing. In other words, you must motivate an Easygoing or Sedate dog with your excitement and enthusiasm. An Easygoing dog may seem to be resisting your authority. Do not confuse his laid-back style with opposition. He's not holding back, he's resting. Teaching *Heel* to a slow-moving dog can be irritating. Stay calm and get into your dog's state of mind.

During the teaching process use lots of body movement. Don't stop moving. First, walk fast, then run a bit, and then slow down to a deliberate walk. Keep changing your pace and your style of movement. Let the dog try to figure out what your next move is going to be. This will keep his attention on you, where it belongs. A dog that pays attention learns better and faster.

Your tone of voice should be varied. Use a number of vocal tones such as happy, subdued, calm, energetic. Do not stop talking to your dog as you go through training motion, and be very happy, enthusiastic, and encouraging. Do not use any voice corrections because they may be too upsetting. Praise works much better for a low-key dog. Do not give dogs of this temperament leash corrections. The leash should be used as a tool for guiding the dog to the right position. Interestingly, distractions are good for dogs of this temperament, and the more distractions, the better. You may train him indoors or out. It's your call.

If your dog has an Aggressive temperament, you can never let down your guard. You must constantly stay aware that the dog may have a dangerous reaction to any of the training procedures. If your dog is aggressive, you must avoid making direct eye-to-eye contact. A direct stare into a dog's eyes is an unmistakable challenge as far as the dog is concerned. It is part of their natural behavior, and pertains to who is top dog in the pack, or in your case, the family.

You must think about how you use your hands in relation to how the dog may respond to them. If your dog was ever hit by someone's hand, or with any object such as a broom handle or a rolled-up newspaper, he will at the very least cringe when someone tries to touch him, and at worst he may bite any hand that comes near him. By all means, be careful and move slowly. It is possible to recondition the dog and get him to respond normally to your hands by gentle stroking, speaking in a soothing tone of voice, and being very loving in general. Do this at every opportunity possible and do it right away. An aggressive dog must be reconditioned this way whether you are training him or not.

How to use your tone of voice depends on the dog's age and if he is Dominant-Aggressive or Fear-Aggressive. A Dominant-Aggressive puppy between the ages of seven weeks and six months requires a firm tone of voice without harshness. A Dominant-Aggressive dog between six and ten months requires an authoritative tone of voice. Use a soft tone of voice that is still firm enough to correct a Fear-Aggressive puppy between the ages of seven weeks and six months. Fear-Aggressive dogs between six and ten months need to hear a firm tone of voice that is not harsh. A professional dog trainer should evaluate aggressive dogs past ten months of age.

A voice correction may not be effective without a leash correction at the same time. Depending on the level of aggression in the dog, voice corrections may not be effective at all. This is why it is important to always have your aggressive dog on a leash during the training sessions. Enthusiastic praise must follow all corrections so the Aggressive dog will accept the correction without reacting to it.

Leash corrections for Aggressive dogs are a bit unpredictable. Be ready for anything when you jerk the leash of an Aggressive dog. His response to a correction could be to jump on you, or to attempt to bite your hand or leg. When beginning the teaching procedures for *Heel*, let the dog run ahead, then stop and administer a leash correction but do not turn around as instructed earlier. Do not turn your back on him. Let him go to the end of the leash as you stand facing him, then jerk the leash. He may try to bite the leash or hold it down with his paws. Slacken the leash and praise the dog if it gets him to stop pulling ahead. Heap lavish praise on the dog and do not hold back, but do not pet him as you do this. Then you may turn in the opposite direction and go into the rest of the *Heel* command as detailed earlier. You must be firm with the dog and establish control over him so you command his respect. With Aggressive dogs you must always have control over them and not back down from anything you demand of them. Do not let the dog know you are frightened of him, if that's the case.

How you give leash corrections depends on the dog's age, size, and level of aggression. What form does the aggression take? Does the dog bully you or other humans? Does he growl, snarl, or curl his lip? Puppies between seven weeks and six months should be corrected with quick, firm jerks that are not too hard. Correct dogs between six and ten months with quick, firm leash corrections. Sometimes you have to give slightly harder corrections at that age, but it really depends on the dog and how aggressive he is.

Always correct a dog right away if he behaves aggressively. Do not wait, and do not hesitate. He must be corrected continuously until he stops behaving aggressively. You should be able to correct and get most of the dog's aggressive behavior under control this way unless he is extremely aggressive. You must remember that it is only safe to correct an aggressive dog until the age of ten months. Past ten months he could be dangerous and certainly unpredictable for those inexperienced with this kind of dog. A professional dog trainer must evaluate dogs past ten months. Train the aggressive dog in a secluded area with no audience or distractions. You might want to consider having this type of dog trained by a professional.

How to Teach Your Dog the *Automatic Sit*

Somewhere near the first page I promised to get into this thing with the weird name. The Automatic Sit sounds like a new computer thing doesn't it? The Automatic Sit is when your dog responds to a stop when walking in *Heel* by going directly into a *Sit* position. The dog will stop every time you do, and *Sit* without being commanded to do it. See, not so complicated is it? So why don't we just call it something simple like "He sits when you stop." I don't know. This is the name of the thing, and I didn't invent it, so we'll stick with what we have.

The way this command is accomplished is simple. All you have to do is let the dog know that you are going to stop, and you do that by just slowing down! Your change in pace alerts him to the fact that there is going to be a change of some kind. If he is paying attention to you, as he should, he will slow down, too. You can give the dog some cues to let him know you are slowing down. Scrape or tap your feet and make a noise. Pull up on the leash as if it were the reins of a horse. Say the dog's name. Make a vocal sound such as clicking your tongue or twittering your lips. You can always snap your fingers. It is all a matter of association. If you do any of these things as you slow down your pace, that noise will become a permanent signal to the dog. Whatever you choose to do for this purpose, you must get the dog's attention with it.

After slowing down for a few seconds, come to a full stop and say, *Sit*. Do not use the dog's name on this command. Saying the command is only done during the teaching process but is not used afterwards. When teaching the Automatic Sit, use the Pushing Technique described earlier. Find the hip joints of your dog's hindquarters and gently squeeze them as you push down with your left hand. Pull the leash up slowly with your right hand until the dog is actually sitting.

Keep repeating this until the dog learns it. If he fails to sit, give him a leash correction and say *Sit* firmly as a reminder. Praise the dog after he successfully obeys each command, even if he did so after a correction. Always, always praise the dog.

Sometimes a dog will not sit at all. It doesn't matter. You must not say the command more than once. Make this a firm rule throughout the training. Do not put yourself in the ridiculous position of training your dog and repeating the command *Sit* over and over until everybody is either laughing at you or until you get sick to your stomach. The dog may never obey you in that situation. Only a leash correction and a demanding tone of voice saying *No* gets the job done. That is what must be done to get the dog to sit for you. And of course, praise him for obeying.

Slow down your pace and gradually come to a full stop. If the dog does not sit, give the command to sit. If he does not respond, give him a leash correction and repeat the word *Sit!* If he responds properly, praise him with enthusiasm, even though he was corrected. This is his motivation. In that rare instance when the dog does not respond to the leash correction accompanied by *No*, give him another correction and the command *Sit.* I don't usually suggest giving the command word with the correction. It causes the dog to associate a negative reinforcement with that particular command. In this extreme situation, though, it becomes necessary. If you give the leash correction properly the first time, you can avoid this problem. One or two firm corrections save time and frustration for everyone. The dog will know you mean what you say when the leash correction is firm. Remember that *Sit* is a command word and *No* is a verbal correction. Although the commands should be given with authority, the corrections should be given with a stronger tone of voice.

The lesson should end once the dog has completed the command successfully for the first time and you should close on a high note. Do not expect the dog to be perfect for several weeks. But the first time he performs the new command correctly, end the lesson and give him lots of praise. If this reward of exuberant praise is generous enough, the dog will remember what he has just learned and will be motivated to look forward to performing properly the next time. Make training sessions fun by showing your dog some enthusiasm for what's going on.

The training variations for the Automatic Sit are the same for dogs of different temperaments and involve the same variations that are found in *Sit*.

"So that about wraps it up for *Heel* and the Automatic Sit, doesn't it?" asks Larry.

"No, it does not. Larry, would you come over here, please?"

The shorter of the two dog owners comes forward almost obediently.

"What's up, Uncle Matty?"

"You know, Phil put his ego out on the line and tried to do one of the lessons with Brownie, and I think it's only fair that you do the same."

Larry smiles and shakes his head.

"Is this some kind of a trap? Am I supposed to screw up just to balance things out with Phil? Is that the idea?"

"No. But you are the dog person of the two of you and I think you deserve a chance to show us what a lifetime of dogs has accomplished, don't you?"

"Oh, sure. I really believe that. Okay. I'll accept your

challenge and prove that I know a thing or two," says Larry as he brings the dog up close to Matty. "What do you want me to do?"

"I want you to teach Brownie the Automatic Sit. Can you do it?"

"Sure."

Larry places Brownie at his left side and he and the dog stand facing the same direction. Larry holds the leash correctly and then begins.

"Brownie, heel."

Both man and dog step off and start walking down the street. Larry walks about a quarter of a city block and starts to turn to his right to command the dog.

"Brownie, heel."

They both turn and come back toward Matty. As Larry approaches, he begins to slow down and finally stops. He looks at the dog, bends over, and places the fingers of his left hand on Brownie's hip joints and starts to squeeze them.

Larry says, "Brownie, sit. Oh, no. No name on *Sit*, right?"

Matty shrugs and offers no help. Larry begins to develop beads of sweat on his upper lip.

"Sit, Brownie. No, forget 'Brownie.' Ah, just sit. Right? Yes, that's it, sit. Brownie, sit. Damn, Brownie. No, not you. I take that back. Sit. That's it, just Sit."

The dog looks up at him and stares blankly into his face.

"So sit. Sit. Sit. Sit!"

The dog yawns and lies down on the pavement and rolls over on his side and tries to sleep.

"Brownie, sit. Damn. I mean Sit. Come on, Sit." He looks at his dog trainer helplessly and says, "I guess loving dogs is different than training dogs, isn't it?"

Both Matty and Phil smile and nod.

"Both you guys have learned a lot today. You know what? I think this is another beginning of a beautiful friendship. Uncle Matty's so proud."

Six
Stay a While

Sitting and Staying

You're walking down the street and you run into a friend, a good-looking friend. You want to get something going. But you know in your heart that it's not going to happen because when Twyla gets wind of it, she's going to blow her top. She demands your undivided attention and never allows another person to get in the way of what she wants. If you stop and talk for more than one minute, she becomes petty and rude and starts pawing at you and pulling you away. It doesn't take long to smell trouble. If that doesn't get you to leave and look at her, she makes this awful sound. It looks like a yawn but sounds like a groan. It is a painfully annoying noise that comes from deep in her throat and is a direct demand for your attention. She is possessive but I'm sure you know all about that. That Twyla. What a dog. Who can resist her, though?

Getting any dog to sit, and to automatically sit is all well and good. But guess what? It's not enough. You need more than that. What we all need is a dog that will not only sit on command but also *Stay* on command and not budge until you say it's okay. So, the next command to teach is logical. You need your dog to obey the command *Stay*. The thing is, *Stay* requires more time and patience to teach than most other commands. Dogs take everything you say for its obvious meaning and do not understand anything between the lines. If you say to your dog in your best leader-of-the-pack voice *Sit*, she will sit, but only for a few seconds, until something catches her attention or she has an itch. Why should your dog feel bad about this? After all, she did obey your command. From her point of view, she did what you wanted. If you expect her to remain in a sitting position longer than a few seconds without the command *Stay*, then you haven't been paying attention to your dog. You have to teach your dog *Stay* to get her to hold her position on your command. This command piggybacks onto the *Sit* command and the *Down* command, making it either *Sit-Stay* or *Down-Stay*. We'll deal with *Sit-Stay* in this chapter.

All right. I want to introduce you to Betty and her six-month-old cocker spaniel, Twyla.

"Thank you, Matthew."

"Excuse me. Did you say something?"

"I said thank you, Matthew."

"I'm sorry but I can't hear you. Would you please speak up."

"How's this?"

"Not much better, could you crank it up just a bit more, please?"

"Okay. This is a loud as I can get. God, my voice just isn't that large. This hurts my chest."

"Oh, please, everyone can speak louder if they need to. I suppose I can hear you now, sort of."

"Well I hope we settled that. I don't know why I'm here, but I guess I'd like to get on with it, please."

"You're here, Betty, because you want Twyla trained and because you have a problem with her, right?"

"Yes."

"Okay, now we're getting somewhere. What's Twyla's problem? Or is it really your problem?"

"Oh, Matthew, why don't you do the talking."

"Betty, your voice is fading again. Okay. I'll do the talking for both of us. But only for a while.

"This is Betty and her dog, Twyla. Betty is a pretty woman, about five feet, three inches, who lives in a small house in the San Fernando Valley, on the other side of Los Angeles. Twyla is the second dog in her life. She had one when she was a child. What I like about Betty is that she is a happy person who smiles most of the time and is mild-mannered. But she has a problem about speaking up. She is never going to scare anybody with a loud, booming voice. She is very sensitive and is very much like Twyla. Their personalities go well together. They are both very sweet."

"Don't forget to tell them I was a dancer, Matthew."

"So you decided to talk. Okay. Please finish the introduction."

"Oh, I think you're doing just fine."

"The only problem with Betty is that her voice is very soft. She barely whispers. I keep saying, 'What, Betty? What are you saying? I can't hear you. Talk louder.' She says, 'I am talking louder.' No you're not, I say. Betty is in her early forties. Her kids are grown up and on their own, and Twyla is the new kid in the house. It's just the two of them. I like and admire her. Betty works all day as a personal secretary but comes home for lunch to take care of Twyla and give her what she needs at midday and make sure she's okay. She loves that dog and wants to do the very best for her. If she could, she would quit her job and just stay home with her, isn't that right?"

"Yes."

"What?"

"Yes, yes, yes!"

"Hey, you don't have to shout. I can hear."

"And I can talk. I owe it to my dog to give her the best education possible, and that's why you're here. Eventually, I want to enter her in dog shows and agility competition. I'd like to do it all."

"Wow. I'll do my best for both of you. I promise. So, what's the problem with Twyla that you're so concerned about?"

"Well, Matthew, I'm worried she is going to run out the front door. She's always ready to go. She ran out of the car once when I opened the door and she was almost killed. That scared me to death. I love to drive. I have friends throughout California, and I want to be able to take Twyla with me in the car when I visit them. This is a frightening concern, and of all the things you are teaching her, I want to stop her from running out the door, any door."

"Well, Betty, you are talking to the right trainer. We are going to teach you and Twyla all about the command *Stay*. It's not enough for a dog to obey the command *Sit*. She has to know *Stay*, too."

"You know, I always thought that if you can make a dog

sit, she would stay there. Now I understand. It's two sepa-rate commands, isn't it?"

"Betty, we have a lot of ground to cover, so let's get started."

How To Teach Your Dog *Stay*

Okay, here's what the command *Stay* is all about. After you give the dog the command *Sit*, she assumes a sitting posi-tion. So what else is new? Typically, her body is upright, her front legs stand straight, and her rear weight rests on her haunches. The dog's hind legs are folded under her flanks and keep the front of her body erect. She looks straight ahead and moves very little, if at all. After being given the proper verbal command and hand signal for *Stay*, she must hold the position until you release her.

The advantages of this command should be obvious. What dog owner doesn't need to be able to get his or her dog to sit still and not move around at certain times, and in certain situations? From your point of view, this is the greatest thing you can teach your dog to do. When some-one is at the door and you put the dog in *Stay*, she will not run out and put her life in jeopardy. When you're cook-ing, when you're on the phone, or when you are enter-taining, you will use this command frequently, and you'll be glad to have it at your disposal. It's so useful to be able to prevent the dog from moving around while you do something else. From the dog's point of view, however, the feeling is different. No dog wants to stay in the same posi-tion when there is something more interesting to see or do. They are like kids; they get restless very quickly.

Some dogs will dash out the door the minute you open it for any reason. Putting the dog in *Sit-Stay* prevents that. Just telling the dog to *Sit* isn't enough. If she knows it as a command she'll obey, but only for a very short while. As soon as you open the door, she'll be out of the house. Ah, but if you taught your dog *Stay,* you wouldn't have so much to worry about. When you're going out, you put the dog in *Sit-Stay.* Just as you are closing the door you release her from the command by saying *Okay.* Then you close the door. And that's all there is to it. Sounds easy, doesn't it? But teaching this command requires a lot patience, diligence, time, and effort on your part. The good news is that every dog I have ever trained learned *Stay* and learned it well. I know you can do it.

Obeying this command is not easy for a dog. Dogs living in the wild within a pack never have to hold a position for very long, even if the leader of the pack is threatening. Remaining in the Stay position goes against every instinct the dog has. They do not enjoy *Sit-Stay. Down-Stay,* holding a position while lying down, is easier on the dog. Of course, moving around and doing anything you want is even easier so we're not going down that road. Because dogs don't like to hold a *Sit-Stay* for a long time, you must not abuse the privilege. Once you teach your dog to obey this command you should not expect her to hold the position forever. *Down-Stay* is for longer periods. A well-trained dog should not be expected to remain in the Sit-Stay position for more than five minutes, maybe a little more.

I have to qualify this whole thing: A dog that has been taught this command will hold the position for a reasonable time. But don't expect miracles if you put the dog in a situation that is too overwhelming. There are going to be times when it's impossible for the dog to obey. Suppose there's a party going on in your home. Unless you put your dog in a straitjacket, she is going to break the command and join the party. Your choices are to take her to a neighbor's house or let her mingle. You might try putting her in a dog crate, but I guarantee she will whine, bark, and carry on. You must not expect her to remain in a stay position for eternity.

The command *Stay* is meant for you to use indoors only. If you should ever use the command outdoors, you must have your dog on a leash and the leash in your hand. There is nothing a dog loves better than to be outdoors, free to roam and explore. And it is every dog owner's fantasy that his or her pet can run around without a leash and, as if by magic, avoid the traffic, dog fights, and all the possible dangers that lurk outdoors for a dog off-leash. Do not be fooled by your dog's ability to stay safe off-leash. It only takes one mistake for life to end.

Sit-Stay can be taught indoors with a six-foot leash or outdoors (in a fenced backyard) also with a six-foot leash. This command is very demanding on both you and the dog, so you must teach the dog in a place that has no distractions.

The goal of this command is to teach your dog to stay while she is in the Sit position until you release her from the command. To teach this command you will need a training collar and a six-foot leather leash. The command involves three techniques: a verbal command, a hand signal that blocks the dog's vision, and a pivotal turn on the ball of your left food.

The Hand Signal. Hold the leash with your right hand. Flatten your left hand with all fingers close together, as if you were going to swim. Say **Stay** and place your left hand in front of the dog's eyes, not closer than four inches. The hand signal blocks his vision for one or two seconds.

Photos by Pam Marks.

The Verbal Command

Position the dog on your left side, so both of you are facing in the same direction. Say the command *Sit* in a firm tone of voice. Praise the dog. Say the command *Stay* in a firm voice and once again praise the dog. Because this is not an action command where the dog moves forward, do not use her name. The leash is held in the right hand. Praise her after she goes into the proper position. Next, give her the command *Stay*. The hand signal is given as you say the verbal command. Once again, praise the dog.

The Hand Signal

Hold the leash with your right hand and allow enough to drape across your knees so there is a little slack plus the width of your body. The signal is given with the left hand. Flatten your left hand and keep all fingers straight and close together as if you were swimming. As you say the command *Stay,* place your left hand in front of the dog's eyes, leaving about four inches of space so you never touch them. The hand signal is accomplished quickly and merely blocks the dog's vision for two or three seconds. Do not touch her eyes. Return your left hand to your side after blocking the dog's vision. Eventually, the dog will remain in the Stay position with the use of the hand signal exclusively. The hand signal is given simultaneously with the voice command.

Turning on Your Left Foot

This is a pivotal turn that allows you to face the dog without causing her to leave the Sit position. To accomplish this, use your left foot as a pivot to rotate yourself in

Turning on Your Left Foot. Your left foot remains in place and swivels as you step off with your right foot and turn to face the dog. Keep the leash above the dog's head. After placing your right foot on the ground, move your left foot next to it so you have made a complete turn and are now facing the dog. You may lower the leash slightly, but keep it tight. Stand in front of the dog for about thirty seconds while he remains in the Stay position. Praise him generously for his correct response.

Photo by Pam Marks.

place. Do not move your foot from its original position. It's okay if the left foot moves a little; nobody can help that. Step off with your right foot and turn to face the dog. Allow your left foot to revolve in place without losing its position as your right foot moves forward by one step. That means you are just about facing the dog. At the same time that you turn around, keep the leash above the dog's head, holding it to one side so you do not hit her on the chin. Keep the leash tight enough to restrain the dog's movements. After you have placed your right foot on the ground, and you are facing the dog, move your left foot next to it so both feet are together. Lower the leash slightly, but keep it tight. You have now accomplished the complete turn and should be facing the dog, eyeball to eyeball. Stand in front of the dog for about thirty seconds while she remains in the *Stay* position. Praise her generously for her correct response. If you do this any other way than the way I just described, the dog will assume you are about to say *Heel* and start moving. The pivotal turn is merely a teaching tool and will not be used after the dog has learned the command completely.

This technique works well if you exercise the proper leash control necessary to hold the dog in place. This is the most important part of teaching the command. As you pivot in front of your dog, hold about eighteen inches of the leash straight up so the leash and collar are high on her neck. The remainder of the leash dangles in a slackened loop from the bottom of your right hand. In this position, the dog cannot move as you turn to face her. What you are doing is holding her in a fixed position with the extended leash. If the leash is held properly, the dog will be under your control and will hold the position until she learns to do it without being held in place. Do not hold the leash too tightly or she may choke, or become frightened and struggle.

The leash is comparable to the reins of a horse. It is an important means of communicating what you want by sending messages and at the same time holding your dog in place. Although it is extended upward, it does not tighten unless the dog tries to move out of the position. The moment he stops moving, loosen up a bit. A horse respects a rider the minute he is mounted if the rider knows how to handle the reins firmly and with authority. The same applies to a dog. If an owner is in control with the use of the leash and collar, the dog will respect her and submit to her authority. The minute the dog observes a lack of consistent control, she is likely to disobey. In turn, the owner will get frustrated and angry and the lesson will end.

The command *Stay* is communicated in the most practical way if your leash control is strict and accurate during the pivotal turn. The entire movement must be completed swiftly and smoothly so your dog does not have time to do anything else like turn or walk. Hold her in place as you get in front of her with an economy of movement. Expect to do this at least ten or fifteen times before she understands what you want. You must praise your dog each and every time you have completed the turn and she has remained in position, even though she had to be held there with the leash. Do not use her name this time when praising her. If you do, she will move out of the position.

"Betty, would you like to try this with Twyla?"

"Oh, Matty. Do I have to?"

"Not if you don't speak any louder than that. And not if

you don't mind that the dog will never obey a command from you."

"Alright. Is that loud enough for you?"

"Yes. Now let me see what you've learned."

Betty takes the leash from Matty's hand and holds it with her right hand. She walks Twyla away from him, then turns around and stands facing him with the dog at her left side. She takes in a large breath of air and speaks to the dog in a loud and clear voice.

"Sit."

Twyla looks up at her and lowers her body in a good sitting position.

"Good girl. *Stay!*"

Betty places her flattened left hand in front of Twyla's eyes for two seconds and pulls it away.

"That's mommy's baby. What a sweetheart. Mommy loves you and wants . . ."

"Betty, Betty. That's enough praise already. You're making a speech. Just get on with it."

"Sorry."

Like the dancer she once was, she stretches her legs with a ballet step. While her feet remain flat on the floor with her toes facing out at the sides she bends her legs and lowers her entire body to the ground in a straight line. Matty looks at her.

"What are you doing?"

"Oh, I'm just getting ready for the rest of this command. In dance they call this a *plié*. It's a good stretching movement."

"Okay. Here we go."

Betty steps forward with her right foot and moves one large step forward but begins to turn to her left as she does this. Her right foot stays in one place but revolves as her body twists around

*toward the dog. She now faces the dog and brings her left foot to
her right foot.*

"What about the leash? Control the dog with the leash,
Betty."

"Damn, I forgot. What do I do now?"

"Control the dog with the leash. Better late than never."

*She raises the leash with her right and left hand together and
brings it up over the dog's head about eighteen inches.*

"Good. Now praise her."

"Ah, good girl, Twyla. You're terrific."

"Okay but don't use the dog's name when you're praising her. It'll make her move."

"What do I do now, Matty?"

"You were very good for the first time. Now hand me
the leash and I'll do the rest."

Backing Off

This is a major part of teaching your dog to *Stay*. You
now have to back off, so to speak. By that, I mean you back
away as the dog remains in the Stay position. This is not as
easy as it sounds because you are trying to teach the dog to
hold her position as you move back. It is important to be
sure that the dog has accepted the demanding leash control that you have imposed.

Begin by saying the command *Stay* and giving the hand
signal. Make the pivotal turn so you are standing directly
in front of the dog. Slowly back away three feet from the
dog. The goal is to teach her to remain in *Sit-Stay* from a
distance of three feet until she is released from the command. Hold the leash about eighteen inches above the
dog's head, then shift it to your left hand, placing your
thumb inside the loop at the top. Your right hand then

Backing Away to Three Feet and Then Backing Away to Six Feet. While holding the leash above the dog's head, slide the leash through your right hand as it is held firmly by the left so it gets longer as you move backward. If the dog walks toward you as you move back, say **Stay,** and move quickly toward him.

Pull the leash through your right hand as you move forward and
hold it once again above the dog's head. Once the dog has
stopped moving, praise him. Pause for several seconds and then
begin backing away again.

Photos by Pam Marks.

grasps the main line of the leash about halfway down, and holds it loosely, directly under the left hand. As you back away, the leash should be able to slide freely through the right hand, allowing it to extend, which will prevent any slack from developing as you back away.

As you back away from the dog, the leash slides through your right hand as it is held firmly by the left and gets longer as you move backward. The dog may begin to walk toward you as you move back. If she does, give her the command, *Stay*, and move in toward her. Pull the leash through your right hand as you move forward and hold it once again above the dog's head. The leash must always be taut so it forces the dog to remain in the Sit position. This is important. If the leash slackens, you will be unable to force the dog to remain in *Sit-Stay*. Always pull the leash slightly to the side as you move in so you do not hit the dog with the metal clip. Stepping toward her will stop her from moving. Once she has stopped moving, she must be praised. Pause for several seconds and then begin backing away again. Keep moving until she tries to move. You may get back a little farther this time. If she moves, step toward her again, say *Stay*, and praise her when she stops moving. Pause once again and then start moving back again until you are at the desired three feet away. Repeat the procedure. Repeat this many times, until she no longer moves as you back off to three feet.

You now have to repeat the procedure all over again so the dog will hold her Stay position at the full six feet of the leash. This only sounds boring. Once you start doing this, you will become so concentrated that you won't have time to think about anything except being ready to move in the minute the dog tries to move out of her Stay position. This will take all your concentration. Keep moving back until the dog tries to move. You may get back farther each time. Repeat the procedure. Step in toward the dog as you pull the leash through your right hand, keeping it taut and above the dog's head. Praise her for stopping and wait several seconds before moving away. Continue this technique until you can back away the full six feet of the leash while the dog continues to sit in *Stay*. Once the dog will remain in position for the entire length of the leash, repeat the process at least fifteen times or more. You are now ready for the next step. See I told you this is complicated.

Walking Around Each Side of the Dog

The point to this step in the lesson is to program the dog so you can walk around her, while she remains in *Stay* without moving. Once she has been given the command *Stay*, the dog must not turn her body around to watch you when you walk to her right or her left side. Most dogs will turn their heads to watch and that is somewhat okay, although it's not perfect for this command. The dog must never be allowed to move her body around once she has been put in *Stay*, or the discipline of this command will break down and it will no longer be reliable.

Start out by placing your dog in the Sit position. Say *Sit*. Praise her. Then say *Stay* and use the hand signal in front of her eyes as you execute the pivotal turn, holding the leash tautly eighteen inches above her head. Praise her.

Step once or twice to the right side of the dog as you hold her in place with good leash control. Return to the original position directly in front of the dog. Now step once or twice to the left side of the dog as you continue to hold her in place with firm leash control. Return to the original position. Repeat this forty or fifty times, or until you can do it without the dog moving her body toward you. This will condition the dog to your side movements while she is held in place. Having accomplished everything so far, repeat everything in the entire lesson up to this point five or ten times, until you are convinced that your dog has learned everything.

Walking Around the Dog

The point to this part of the lesson is to teach your dog to remain in *Sit-Stay* and extend her ability to obey the command while you are out of her direct line of sight. As before, with the dog on your left side say *Sit.* Praise her. Give her the next command, *Stay,* and execute the hand signal in front of her eyes. Praise her. Make the pivotal turn and stand in front of her, maintaining eighteen inches of taut leash above her head. Hold the leash with your left hand, and grasp the leash directly underneath it with your right hand. Review all the elements of *Sit-Stay* thus far. Then, turn toward the dog, and back away from her to the end of the leash. During the procedure, keep reminding her to *Stay,* praising her after each reminder as a reward for obeying. Keeping the leash high and taut, move a foot to the right, then stop and praise the dog. Reverse directions and move to the left, increasing the distance to two feet. Praise the dog with a soft, soothing tone for staying in position.

Continue moving from right to left, gradually increasing your distance in each direction. The dog is permitted to turn her head to follow your movements, but not her body. At this phase, the dog's tendency is often to twist her body around to watch what you are doing. If she tries to turn, you must stop her. Step forward, tighten the leash, and say *Stay,* followed immediately with praise such as "Good girl."

When you have reached a 180-degree angle, walk back and forth from side to side twelve times. Let your dog know how much her performance has pleased you.

Next, slowly start walking around her, with the intention of making a full circle. At frequent intervals, call out to her to *Stay,* and tell her how good she is. If she moves, tighten up on the leash and say *Stay.* Reassure the dog with a cool tone of voice, offering praise and encouragement. Take large steps. Work the leash with finesse as you extend it when you are behind the dog and take it back in as you come around to her front. Never allow any slack in the leash and maneuver it so you maintain absolute control over the dog. Tighten the leash every time the dog tries to move, and release it slightly when she settles down. Praise her every time she settles down. The key to your control during your circling of the dog is firm leash control and praise. When the dog tries to move out of the Stay position, quickly pull up on the leash, reminding her to *Stay.*

Leash control is everything. It helps the dog develop respect for your authority. The thought of the leash remains in the dog's mind for her entire life as a symbol of your control. The dog will always think of herself as connected to the leash even when it is not on her. When you have completed a full circle around the dog, stop and praise her.

Teaching *Stay* is hard on your dog and on you, too. I suggest you do not attempt to teach the entire command in one session. Sometimes it takes several sessions for the dog to get accustomed to your pivot. When teaching more than one phase of this command in one day, rest one hour between each phase. Do not teach more than two sessions a day. Dogs tire and bore easily, and after a point, they lose their ability to pay attention. Take all the time necessary for the dog to absorb all the steps completely. If you go too fast, the dog may please you by performing well the first time, but then fail to remember what was taught the next day. It is well worth the effort to be patient and teach each phase of this command slowly and carefully and with all the repetitions suggested.

Alone in a Room

One of the most useful applications of *Stay* is when you want the dog to remain in a room while you leave it for a short period of time. Teaching this requires the six-foot leash and the training collar.

Once the dog has learned the command *Sit* and *Sit-Stay*, place the dog in *Sit* and drop the leash to the floor. Using the verbal command and the hand signal place the dog in *Stay*. Walk out of the room. Reenter the room after five seconds. Praise the dog if she did not move. Repeat this about twenty times. Next, extend the length of time that you are out of the room. Do it for a ten-second absence. Praise the dog if she did not move and repeat this twenty times. Keep increasing the time that you are out of the room until you can leave her alone for five minutes. Always let the leash remain connected to the dog's collar even though you are not there to hold it. The leash should now be a symbol of your authority and should serve you well.

Practice this form of *Stay* by putting it to everyday use.

Leave the dog alone in a room and have someone ring the doorbell. If the dog runs to the door, give her a leash correction with a sharp *No!* Don't forget the immediate praise after the leash correction. There are dozens of situations that come up every day in which you can practice this command. One way to test the dog is to extend the six-foot leash to its fullest length and execute quick, gentle tugs as you say *Stay* with each tug. If the dog remains in *Stay* even though she is being pulled along, she has learned the command very well.

Sit-Stay for Dogs of Different Temperaments

If your dog has a High-Energy temperament, I'm sure it won't come as a surprise that she is just not going to want to sit still while you try to teach her this command. She is going to want to walk away. Like most dogs, she wants to be with you. Nevertheless, you have to try to relax her so she'll hold the *Stay* position in the course of the lessons. That's a tough demand for a High-Energy dog. You must be patient, steady, and remain calm, even when the dog tests you. Dogs like this are going to be restless. Their energy is endless so try to calm the dog down and cut into some of that energy before the lesson by exercising her. Get out there and run the dog, or toss a ball or a Frisbee, or go for a long walk. Do anything that gets the dog working. The idea is to use up some of the animal's energy before each lesson. You must be patient.

Body language comes into play here. Do not move about too quickly. Go in the opposite direction of your dog's energy level. Move in a slow, deliberate manner while maintaining firm control of the leash. Do not make sudden moves. Block the dog's unnecessary movements with your body. Your voice should sound determined and be supported with some authority. Commands should be spoken in a clean, precise way and should always be followed by praise given in a subdued manner. If you are too energetic or too enthusiastic, especially with your praise, the dog is likely to lose her ability to concentrate and will try to play with you.

Voice corrections should be spoken in a quick, authoritative, no-nonsense way. Praise the dog after each correction, but in a subdued manner. It's a shame to hold back your enthusiasm, but if you don't, you'll never teach *Stay* to your dog. Leash corrections should consist of a quick, firm snap of the leash so your dog does not misunderstand. The snap of the leash must make the point and match your voice correction.

Train your High-Energy dog in a quiet, undisturbed place, such as your home, your back yard, or your apartment. This is necessary until the command has been mastered. Take your dog outside to practice once she has learned the command. It is just as important to practice the command while exposed to normal daily distractions. It's tricky but clear.

If your dog has a Shy temperament, try to figure out what form the shyness takes. What exactly is your dog shy about? Noise? New places? Strangers? Other dogs? Think about what it takes to learn *Sit-Stay,* consider which conditions will make it difficult for your dog to learn this command, then try to avoid those conditions.

Try to see the situation from your dog's point of view in relation to her shyness. Once you get the picture, it will be easier for you to be patient and compassionate and come up with a workable approach to the training. For example, the way you carry yourself could make your Shy dog feel better when you train her. Do not move too suddenly. A Shy dog becomes very nervous when a tall person stands too close. The body language in that situation is just too overbearing. Many of us use our hands in dramatic ways to express ourselves. But, a Shy dog may be nervous about fast-moving hands. Slow down and make fewer and smaller gestures. Some Shy dogs cannot bear to be even three feet away from their owner. Do nothing that encourages your dog to stay too close to you or makes her move toward you.

Your tone of voice is very important to a dog of this temperament. Soften your voice and try to sound reassuring and understanding. Your dog may not understand the exact meaning of your words, but she will certainly respond appropriately to the sound. When you praise her, be generous and take every opportunity to use praise as a way to encourage the dog. Teaching the specifics of a command is far more effective with a Shy dog than resorting to corrections, especially if you are harsh in any way. Go over the lessons as often as is necessary. If you must correct your dog, rely more on voice corrections than leash corrections. Do not say *No* with the same emphasis that you would with a dog that isn't shy. Be gentle. Voice corrections must be followed immediately with loving praise.

If a leash correction is really called for, do not be too firm or too harsh. An inappropriate leash correction will damage the training. Keep the leash taut, but do not allow the training collar to tighten too much around the dog's neck. The tension of the leash must not be too great. The more you use the leash to hold the dog in place, the easier the command will be to teach.

Conduct the lessons in your home or in a quiet, se-cluded backyard with no one there to watch. Your dog may also be shy about strange or loud sounds, so you should work in a very quiet area at first, which will make it easier for her to learn. It is a good idea to eventually take the practice sessions out to a busy area with distractions as a positive part of the learning process.

If your dog has a Strong-Willed temperament, she will not cooperate with you in the beginning of *Sit-Stay* lessons. She will not Sit still for you and she certainly won't Stay in one position for you. The dog is going to test your deter-mination. She will try anything and everything to keep from doing this at first. Do not lose your cool. Be patient and rely on the teaching techniques to get the job done. The techniques have proved time and time again to work in most situations for most dogs.

You must strike a balance between maintaining a take-charge attitude and not being too dominant. Show no anger toward the dog at any time, especially during those moments of frustration when the dog refuses to learn. If you become overpowering, you will only succeed in mak-ing the dog stubborn, aggressive, or even shy. Ask yourself what is the dog's point of view. How would you like to be bossed around and bullied? Who can tolerate that much dominance? This can be helped by your tone of voice, which should be firm, authoritative, but without harshness or anger.

Do not use harsh voice corrections. If you try to intimi-date your dog with harshness in the sound of your voice, you will not only fail to make progress with this command, you will also injure the bond you have established with your pet. It will help you find the right tone if you think of

this as a teacher-student situation. Your dog has to understand that you are the teacher and he is the student. You
must also consider yourself the leader of her pack. You
can get the command taught with a firm, but not frightening, tone of voice. Just think about teaching the command
and getting the dog to obey it. Constant verbal repetition
of the command is the way to accomplish that. Leash corrections are important. Hold on to control over the dog
with medium to firm corrections. One solid jerk of the
leash is far more effective in the long run than three or
four mild ones. When the leash corrections are too soft,
you have to give too many of them to correct the dog
properly. Too many corrections, even mild ones, irritate
and intimidate the dog.

Train your Strong-Willed dog in a quiet, secluded
part of your home, yard, or apartment. Do not let any
spectators watch. Once your dog has learned the command, it is desirable and important to practice in the
world where some people are going to watch you both. Do
not be afraid of distractions at this point. They are actually
helpful.

If your dog has an Easygoing or Sedate temperament,
think of her as a loving animal lying on the floor, watching
you become exasperated while you try to teach her this
command. An Easygoing dog probably wonders what all
the fuss is about, because she is not thinking about moving, sitting, or staying or anything. She is just not thrilled
about working for you. But you must never confuse the
Easygoing or Sedate temperament with stupidity. There is
a difference between having a slow body and a slow mind.
Body language is not really an issue here, not yours, not
your dog's. It really doesn't matter how you move your

body. Easygoing dogs do not care. With these dogs you need to make your voice as easygoing as your dog and use a soft tone. Sometimes, however, you may have to use a louder sound so your dog doesn't fall asleep. Keep up your energy to stimulate the dog and avoid falling asleep yourself.

Voice corrections should be softer than usual. You may be firm when necessary, but not harsh. Leash corrections are sometimes necessary. Keep a taut leash on a dog that keeps trying to lie down. That is a real problem with dogs of this temperament. The giant breeds, such as the Saint Bernard, Newfoundland, and Mastiff, are typical of Easygoing or Sedate dogs. If you have one of these dogs, *Sit-Stay* may not work for you. Some dogs are so heavy and so lethargic that *Sit-Stay* is too much of a strain. You always have the option of using *Down-Stay* instead. Where you decide to train a dog of this temperament is not even worth thinking about. You can go indoors or outdoors, and be in an area with or without distractions. It just doesn't matter.

If your dog has an Aggressive temperament, you need to be aware of whatever it is that will make her behave in an aggressive way. Try to figure out what part of teaching this command might set her off. Will it be the tone of your voice or the way you administer leash corrections? How you move or hold your body? What about your teaching style? You must be cautious with a dog that has an Aggressive temperament. This is especially important when you try teaching a command as demanding as *Sit-Stay*. It is necessary to stay aware of your dog's potentially dangerous reactions. This is even more important if your dog has already shown a tendency to bite. If that is the case, you should consider using a soft nylon muzzle for safety's sake.

When working with an aggressive dog, you are advised not to stand over her or make direct eye contact. A direct stare into the eyes of a dog is a challenge as far as the dog is concerned. The issue is dominance. It is important to understand that there are many dominant female dogs as well as males. Do not lean over the dog too much or make her feel cornered. Be especially careful about hand signals and the use of your hands in general throughout the lessons.

Think about how your dog is going to respond to your pushing her into position with your hands. A dog that has been hit with a bare hand or with a rolled-up newspaper may bite anyone who puts his or her hands near her for any purpose. Be cautious and move very slowly when you work with an aggressive dog. Some dogs can be conditioned to respond positively to human hands by being stroked gently and lovingly and spoken to in a soothing tone of voice at the same time. This should be done at every possible opportunity to an Aggressive dog, whether you are training the dog or not.

Be very cautious if your dog has been jerked on a leash too much. A simple leash correction could trigger aggressive behavior. She may react badly to you. Do not be too dominant. Remain alert to how the dog reacts to you when you attempt to train her and watch yourself. Do not get bitten. Be patient, be cool, be smart.

The tone of voice you should use depends on the age of the dog and whether she is Dominant-Aggressive or Fear-Aggressive. A Dominant-Aggressive puppy between the ages of seven weeks and six months requires a firm, but not harsh, tone of voice. For Dominant-Aggressive dogs between six and ten months, use an authoritative, demanding tone of voice. A Fear-Aggressive puppy between seven weeks and six months requires a soft tone of voice that is still firm enough to correct her. For Fear-Aggressive dogs between six and ten months, you need a firm, but not harsh, tone of voice. If your Aggressive dog is past ten months of age, you should get a professional evaluation from a dog trainer or a dog behaviorist.

Voice corrections should be given with a determined attitude and a firm *No*. This is usually effective, but do not forget to praise the dog immediately afterward. Some dogs do not respond properly to a voice correction alone and require a leash correction at the same time. Voice corrections are not effective for all dogs. It's a good idea to keep an Aggressive dog on a leash throughout all training sessions. Make sure you praise your dog after each and every correction. This is extremely important.

Most dog owners are surprised when their dogs growl, snap, or bite after a leash correction. This could be the result of too many leash corrections too harshly given. The dog's age, size, and level of aggression are important factors when giving leash corrections. Is the dog a bully? Does she growl, snarl, or curl her lip? Young dogs between seven weeks and six months of age should be corrected with quick, firm jerks that are not too hard. Dogs between six and ten months should be corrected with quick, firm jerks. They may have to be given with slightly harder tugs at that age. It depends on the dog's level of aggression.

It is not safe to correct an Aggressive dog once she is past ten months of age. Once she approaches that age, she may be too dangerous for a nonprofessional. Such dogs need to be evaluated by a professional dog trainer or an animal behaviorist. Train your Aggressive dog at home.

Take advantage of the privacy of your home and the safety factor. If the dog is going to be upset and become aggressive, you must not endanger innocent bystanders. When teaching this command to your Aggressive dog, do not allow any distractions, such as dogs, kids, or neighbors, to serve as an audience.

"So, what do you think, Betty?"

"It's a bit overwhelming. There's a lot to cover here."

"Yes there is. Do you think it's worth the effort? Tell me what you think. You can tell me. I'm Uncle Matty."

"Okay. I love my dog more than anything else in my life right now, and I know that what we're doing here is not only good for her but could save her life some day. I can see that and I want to do this, no matter how much time and effort it takes. If anything happened to Twyla, I would be devastated. I guess you think I'm silly, don't you?"

"Are you serious? Me? I personally know five thousand people who feel just like that. And you know what? I'm one of them, too. So if you're a fool, then Uncle Matty's a fool, too."

Seven
Common *Down*

Going Down and Staying Down

This command is probably your dog's favorite position, but it's the hardest one for him to learn. Most dogs look forward to their naps and quiet times when they can just lie down on the floor and get some sleep. Family dogs, unlike working dogs, can always be found loafing around and sleeping on the floor. After all, the family dog's job is to eat when you feed him, accept your love when you give it, and play with you when he feels you need the exercise. He is off duty the rest of the time and catches up on his sleep if you don't bother him. So lying down is a good thing if you're a dog. It's not so bad for the rest of us, either. Your dog will watch you from the kitchen floor when you cook dinner, and he won't even bother getting up, unless of course you happen to drop a bit of sirloin on the floor. In the summer, dogs love lying on a cool floor or on fresh grass. So being in the Down position is not a hardship for your dog. It's a normal place to be. From that viewpoint the *Down* command is no big deal. Ah, but learning the command and accepting the teaching process, well, that's another story. Dogs usually do not enjoy that part of it. The reason is not hard to figure out.

If you were to ask any dog which command is his favorite, he would likely tell you it's *Down*, because the position is comfortable. Go ahead, ask any dog and then tell me what he says. He'll say he likes it, but he won't tell you how much he disliked learning the command because the process made him very insecure. It's true, the process is not a comfortable one for dogs. Oh, sure, once he's learned it, he likes the Down position a lot. But during the teaching process the dog must be pushed down to the floor as you give the command, which is something that makes him very uneasy and insecure. Dogs do not normally go into that position unless they feel safe and secure and it's their idea.

When a dog sits or walks, he is on his feet, and that means he can protect himself from just about anything. He can fight if he has to, or he can run, or he can strut about and threaten those imaginary or real enemies. If you make him go down to the floor, he is in his most vulnerable position. It goes against his built-in sense of survival, which has been present since his puppyhood. The position is also a gesture of submission and that's not easy for all dogs. From his point of view, another dog or some kind of threatening creature has the advantage over him. Naturally, that's ridiculous because none of his enemies are going to be marching through your kitchen. But the dog doesn't know that. When you force him to lie down for the first time during the teaching process, you are up against his instinct to protect himself. He thinks that going Down makes him vulnerable. But don't worry. Both you and the dog will get through it. They all do and they all do very well. Some dogs just have a harder time with it than others. There is another issue for many dogs about this command, and I'll get to that in a minute.

"Why not now?" asks Millie Deeter of Springfield, Illinois.

Matthew is taken by surprise.

"Oh, boy. Here we go again. Another voice coming in from off the page. Can't anybody wait until they're invited to speak?"

"Sure. But by then we'll all be feeding the pigeons and comparing Social Security checks. Do you have any idea how much you have to say?"

"Millie, have you had your medication today? You know how you get when you miss a pill. I know I have a lot to say but that's because dog training is more sophisticated than you realize. There's a lot you have to tell people if you're going to teach them how to train their dogs. *Down* is a very involved command to teach, and isn't that why you have me here, by the way? Let's ask that six-foot-three, two-hundred-pound guy over there. You know the one—you're married to him. Yo, Big Dan. Come talk to Uncle Matty."

"Do I have to? Let Millie handle this, okay?"

"You guys are a riot. I come all the way to Springfield just to help you with your *Down* problem and you're raggin' on me about talking too long."

"You wrote to me about your problem with, what's his name?"

"Sparks."

"Yeah, Sparks. He's your best Golden Retriever right?"

Dan gets a hurt expression on his face.

"Sparks is *one* of our best Golden Retrievers, but we can't show him."

Millie cuts in, "He's too hyper for the show ring. You know how the show judges always say of the winning dog 'he asked for it' when they explain how they made their choice? Well, Sparks doesn't ask. He takes it and that's not a good thing. It happened at his first dog show. He snatched the winning rosette right out of the judge's hands and ran out of the ring with the ribbon in his mouth. The problem was he hadn't won. He took another dog's rosette."

Dan adds excitedly, "I thought we'd lost him forever at the Houston Astrodome. What a show hall! It's huge behind all those seats. Have you ever been there?"

"Uh, no, but isn't that a baseball stadium?" asks Matty.

"Baseball? Are you kidding? The Astrodome is for dog shows. Isn't that right, Millie?"

"Well, Dan, I recall something about a baseball team, and some football team that used to play there. But you're right, that's where the big cluster show takes place. It's mostly for dog shows."

Matty leans into his wristwatch. "Hello, Mars to Earth. My work here is finished. I'm ready to go home now."

"Come on, Matthew," says Millie impatiently. "Dan and I have been breeding and showing Golden Retrievers for twenty years. You've seen our trophy room. We've accomplished a lot, and Sparks is a great dog except we can't take him in the ring anymore because he's too spirited. We want to be able to live with him in the house. We need to teach him *Down*."

Dan pipes in.

"Matty, I've trained all our dogs over the years, but this one has me stumped. He'll do all the important commands but I cannot get him to cooperate for the *Down* command. Whatever we do with the other dogs does not work for this one. He's a beautiful dog. A near perfect physical example of a Golden Retriever. I always considered Goldens to be the smartest dogs in the world but I think I just have a dumb dog here."

Matty gets a pained expression on his face.

"I doubt that. There's no such thing as a dumb dog. Maybe your teaching method is wrong. Sometimes owners try to put a round key into a square hole. Dogs have problems and they boil down to dog problems or people problems. I met Sparks and if you can't teach that dog *Down,* then it's a people problem. I'm sure of it. You are applying one-size-fits-all dog training to a dog that's not like your others. I have to tell you that no two dogs are alike, even if they're the same breed and from the same litter. It's not Sparks's fault that you can't teach him *Down.* It's your fault. You have the wrong key."

"I don't know about that, Matty. I've trained a lot of dogs."

"Okay, but it's not working here, is it? Something's wrong. When the teaching doesn't go well it's a people problem. It has to be. Does the dog like to please you?"

"Yes."

"Does he do the other commands for you?"

"Yes."

"And *Down?*"

"No."

"You're frustrated because your training tools are not

working. You just need the right tool for the right job."

"Dan, I tried to tell you that in other words. Remember? I told you we're doing something wrong. So what do we do?" asked Millie.

"It's not that difficult. You alter the training to fit Sparks's personality or temperament. You have to understand that this is a tough command for a dog like Sparks because it becomes a dominant-subordinate issue. He's down there and you're up here in control. Some dogs do not want to give up their position of dominance, so you have to establish your dominance over the dog, but in a way that is neither harsh nor punishing. You can't force the dog to accept this command. You don't want it to become a battle of wills because that makes the owner fall apart. You have to figure out which is the best training method for Sparks. Sparks is a high-energy dog and you need to take that into consideration. I'd give him a vigorous exercise session before beginning each training lesson and tire him out, just to calm him down. Then I'd choose the Dog's Leg Method as the introductory training method for him, involving pulling his front legs forward so he has no choice but to go Down on command. Your tone of voice should be firm but not harsh so the command doesn't sound like *No*. You don't want to scare the dog. Also, you mustn't use his name with the command *Down*, because he associates his name with moving forward and coming to you for affection. You use his name and he is going to move toward you rather than obey the command. When you teach this command to a high-energy dog like Sparks kneel next to him rather than stand over him. Do you get the picture here?"

Both Dan and Millie nod.

Dan says, "So how do I customize this training to Sparks, Matty?"

"Think about your dog and what he is like and then try to figure it all out from his point of view."

Dan nods and says, "I got it. I think I got it."

"Good. Repeat after me, the rain in Spain falls mainly on the plain."

"Oh, you Uncle Matty, you," says Millie as she pretends to hit him on the arm.

"Oh, Matty's proud."

It will help you teach this command if you know what the Down position is supposed to look like. When you give your poochie the command *Down,* he is supposed to lower his body to the ground, or the floor, or the carpet, or wherever. He should be completely relaxed with his head held upright and he should be looking straight at you, waiting for your next command. The dog's front legs should be stretched out in front of him like two straight lines. His rear legs hold his entire body weight. Most dogs prefer to fold their hind legs under their body but others lay them out to the side, which is weird looking because it makes the dog look like he is in a reclining position. I have also seen some dogs stretch their hind legs straight out behind them like a centerpiece at a luau. This is also weird.

The command *Down* can be useful when your dog is into something bad, dangerous, or undesirable—such as going into garbage, running away, jumping on people, or just making a nuisance of himself when you have company. The command by itself is not a remedy for misbe-having. That's what all of dog training is for. But *Down* will keep the dog out of trouble when it is used properly. As I told you in *Sit-Stay*, you cannot use this command to di-rectly stop unwanted behavior. You must first say the com-mand *No*, praise the dog, and then give him the command *Down*, praise him, and then say *Stay*, and then praise him. If you give your commands in that order whenever the dog is misbehaving, you will at least have stopped the problem temporarily. The thing is to then recondition the dog so he doesn't go into the garbage or do whatever it is that you don't like again.

How many times have you used the command *Down* when you meant stop it or don't jump or knock it off? In dog training, language is a precise tool, so you must say ex-actly what you mean or you will confuse the dog and you won't get the desired effect. When you snap *Down* at your dog you are actually saying to him go down on the ground with his head erect, his eyes looking forward, his front legs extended and his hind legs relaxed beneath you.

There are occasions when *Down* and *Down-Stay* com-mands are useful and simply make life better for you. When you're having guests for dinner, it's hard for your dog to leave you and your guests alone. In the *Down* and *Down-Stay*, the family dog can still be part of the doings and yet stay out of everyone's hair. *Down* and *Down-Stay* are also useful outdoors if you want to sit in the park without the bother of a dog yanking on his leash. The reason this command is useful is that if your dog settles down into a comfortable position, he will probably sleep while you read, talk, or do whatever you need to do.

Teaching *Down* includes a hand signal that is an important part of the command. It's very important. The signal requires that you flatten your hand and place your fingers together as though you were going to salute someone. You are asked to make your arm absolutely straight and un-bending and lower it in a steady downward direction with your palm facing the ground. There's more to it but it isn't necessary to deal with all that here. The reason I'm bringing this up now is to let you know the command could be a problem if your dog is hand-shy. In other words, if he's been hit in the past or the present, he is probably going to be upset when you use your hand to teach this command. As your hand comes at him, he may respond aggressively or just flinch out of his fear of being hit again. You may already know this because if the condition exists, he probably has the same response when you try to pet him or brush him or simply touch him. I know you know you're not supposed to hit your dog, for any reason. But I wanted to caution you so you do not get bitten when you try to teach *Down*.

If your dog is hand-shy, it is probably because someone in the past, not necessarily you, abused the dog. It is amazing how many people slap a puppy thinking they are train-ing the dog. If this applies to you, stop hitting him now and we'll go on from there. Your job is to convince your dog you love him and that your hands are only going to be used for good things in the future, such as petting, brush-ing, feeding, and maybe even massaging.

If your dog has been hit over a long period of time, or has been hit severely, then it is too late. He may never be able to respond to a hand signal without fear. If that is the situation, rely on the verbal part of the command exclu-sively. That can work, too, although the hand signal makes things easier. You could recondition your dog by creating new associations with your hands, such as lavishing him with generous praise and affection as you touch him. Start out slow and work your way up to actually using your hands on his body. I have had the experience of turning hand-shy dogs around, but only after being consistent about it for extended periods of time. I'd give you a time frame, but it's different for every dog. But don't give up. A hand-shy dog can eventually be turned around, even if you have to have a professional dog trainer help you. The important thing is take an oath to never hit your dog again and to use your hands only for affectionate praise, expressions of love, and other positive things. You must also eliminate the use of your hands for threats, aggressive or violent gestures, or even accusing the dog by pointing your finger at him. Pointing your finger at the dog and saying "What did you do? Bad dog" causes the same harmful effect. You cannot bond with your dog if you hit him. And you cannot properly train your dog if you do not bond with him.

One more thing before we get to the nuts and bolts of this command. This is a difficult command for your dog to accept. So my advice to you is that you do your teaching alone with your dog. Also, he is not going to learn this in one session. Do not set a time goal. Just take all the time you need, until the dog has learned and accepted the command to your satisfaction.

Shoot for two sessions a day, spaced at about four hours apart. Don't let each session last longer than fifteen minutes because your dog is going to be tired. It is an excellent idea to run your dog through all the other commands he knows before starting each *Down* and *Down-Stay* session.

Believe it or not, by running him through the other commands you will organize his mental processes so he will be ready to learn this new and difficult command. During all the years I have been training dogs, I have found that dogs learn this command the best because you spend more time with it, and because you have to be more diligent than with any of the other commands in the course. These sessions are going to pay off for you because you will use this command more than any other during the course of your day. It's a great feeling to raise your hand in the air with the dog five or ten feet away and watch him obey your hand as it goes down and he goes down. In dog training, it's a thing of beauty. You're going to love it.

How to Teach Your Dog the Command *Down*

This command is difficult to teach and requires an individualized approach. For that reason I am offering you eight different introductory methods to choose from, and I will explain which temperament of dog should be taught with which individual method. Having eight introductory methods to choose from also gives more than enough alternatives if one does not work for your dog. If one doesn't work, try another one that makes sense to you. You may find it to your advantage to use one or two of these methods together. Use your imagination. These introductory methods are numbered from 1 to 8 for the sake of clarity and easy access. Read each method first and then choose which one or more is best for you and your dog. After you finish the work of any one of the eight methods you are far from finished with this command.

The Hand Method.

Photo by Pam Marks.

You must then continue with all the remaining teaching procedures that follow, starting with "Saying *Down* Properly" and ending with "Down for Dogs of Different Temperaments." In other words, once you've finished with one of eight methods, you are *not* finished with teaching this command. You must go on to the rest of the procedures.

1. The Hand Method.

Most dogs can be taught with this method, which is the standard *Down* method. It is the method of choice for dogs with Shy temperaments and/or Easygoing or Sedate temperaments. You must not even consider this method for High-Energy or Aggressive dogs.

Stand by your dog's right side just as you did when you taught him *Heel,* and hold the leash in your right hand. Allow the leash to drape across your legs. Face the same direction as your dog. Say *Sit,* and praise the dog as he goes into the position. Say *Stay,* using the proper hand signal, and once again praise the dog. Get down on your left knee. Say *Down* in a firm tone of voice (see "Saying *Down* Properly," p. 235). Place the middle finger of your left hand between the dog's front paws and hold both paws with that one hand. This will give you a secure grip on both paws with your hand. The idea is to separate his paws with your finger so they cannot be squeezed together, which is potentially painful. Now lift the dog's front paws just a bit with your left hand and move them forward. The dog will slowly but surely lower himself to the ground. He will have no choice.

Praise him generously after he performs the action without resistance each time (see "Praise," p. 236). Do this ten or fifteen times. Keep repeating it until he does not resist you as you place him in the desired position. Sometimes a dog will begin to go down without being placed in the *Down* position.

Please skip the remaining down methods and go directly to "Saying *Down* Properly" (p. 235).

2. The Dog's Leg Method.

Large dogs do well with the Dog's Leg Method. It's also good for dogs whose paws are too thick to manage with one hand. The Dog's Leg Method relies on the leg instead

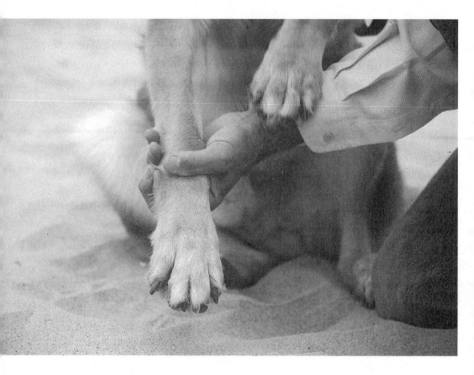

The Dog's Leg Method.

Photo by Pam Marks.

of the paws for moving the dog into a *Down* position. Dogs with High-Energy temperaments, Shy temperaments, Strong-Willed temperaments, and Easygoing or Sedate temperaments can also do well with this method.

Stand next to the dog on his right side, as in *Heel,* and hold the leash in your left hand, allowing it to drape across your legs. Face the same direction as the dog. Say *Sit.* Praise the dog. Say *Stay.* Use the proper hand signal. Praise the dog for holding the position. Go down on your left knee. Give the command *Down.* (see "Saying *Down* Properly" p. 235) and lift the dog's right or left front leg with your right hand. Put the dog in the *Down* position by lifting the right or left front leg and moving it forward. Lift his right front leg forward if he tends to place most of his weight on his right side. If he tends to carry his weight on his left side, then lift his left front leg forward. Praise the dog after each repetition (see "Praise," p. 236). Keep repeating this method at least ten or fifteen times, or until the dog no longer resists being placed in the *Down* position. Some dogs offer no resistance and go down practically on their own. It would be lucky for you if your dog did that. Most dog owners have to repeat this process until the dog finally goes Down on his own.

Skip the remaining methods and move directly to "Saying *Down* Properly" (p. 235).

3. The Push Method

This is an optional method for large dogs that are hard to manage and cannot or will not respond to the other methods. It is also recommended for dogs who have the following temperaments: Shy, Strong-Willed, and Easygoing or Sedate.

Stand by the dog's right side as you would for *Heel*, but hold the leash with your left hand instead of your right. Face the same direction as your dog. Say *Sit*. Praise the

Put your right hand under the dog's belly or behind his front legs. Say **Down**. As you say the command, sweep your right hand forward, from under the dog's belly or from just behind his front legs. Push his legs forward, forcing him to fall gently in the Down position.

Photos by Pam Marks.

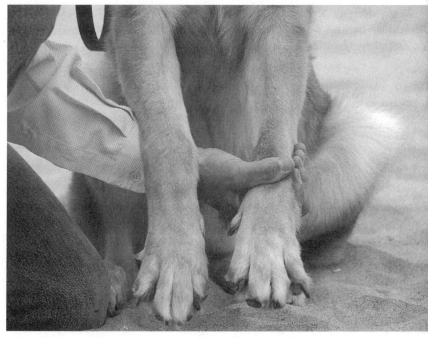

dog for going into the proper position. Say *Stay.* Once again, praise the dog. Kneel down on one knee and hold the leash with your left hand. Put your right hand under the dog's belly as though you were going to hold it or place it right behind his front legs. This is optional. Say *Down* in a firm tone of voice (see "Saying *Down* Properly," p. 235). As you give the verbal command maintain the dog's position by holding the leash taut with your left hand.

Then sweep your right hand forward, either from under the dog's belly or from just behind his front legs. Push his legs forward, forcing him to gently fall into the *Down* position. You are practically lifting his front paws off the ground and pushing them forward. Keep extending your sweeping right hand forward until the dog is in the proper position. Praise him after each repetition (see "Praise," p. 236). If the dog is going to learn this method, you must repeat it ten or fifteen times, until he does not resist being placed in the Down position. He may even go Down without being forced into the position.

Skip the remaining methods and move directly to "Saying *Down* Properly" (p. 235).

4. The Shoulder Method

This method involves pushing the dog's shoulders down to get him into a Down position rather than lifting or lowering him there. This is an effective option and is good for dogs with the following temperaments: High-Energy; Shy; Strong-Willed; Easygoing or Sedate; or Aggressive (if under ten months).

Stand by the dog's right side as in *Heel,* and hold the leash with your right hand. Face the same direction as the

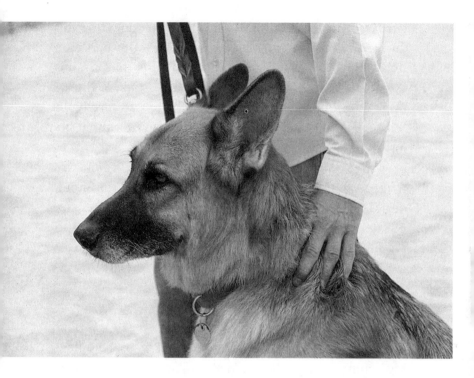

Hold the leash about twelve inches above the dog's head with your right hand and keep it taut. Grip the dog's shoulder blades with the thumb and middle finger of your left hand and push down. Do this as you say **Down.**

Photo by Pam Marks.

dog. Say *Sit.* Praise the dog for going into the proper sit position. Say *Stay* and once again praise the dog. Go down on your left knee or lean over the dog as you continue to face forward. Say *Down* in a firm voice (see "Saying *Down* Properly" p. 235).

Hold the leash about twelve inches above the dog's head with your right hand and keep it taut. Grip the dog's shoulder blades with the thumb and middle finger of your left hand and push down. Do this the same time that you say *Down*. Praise the dog lavishly once he is Down. Always praise him after each repetition (see "Praise," p. 236). It is essential that you repeat this method at least ten or fifteen times or until the dog does not resist being pressured into the Down position. He may begin to go down without being placed in the Down position.

In the event that this method does not work you may try to use a combination of methods. For example, the Shoulder Method mixes well with the Leg Method because applying pressure to the shoulders may not be enough to place the dog into *Down*.

Skip the remaining methods and move directly to "Saying *Down* Properly" (p. 235).

5. The Sliding-Leash Method

This method should only be used on dogs of the following temperaments: Strong-Willed, Easygoing or Sedate, or Aggressive (if under ten months). The Sliding-Leash Method is also effective for extra large dogs that are clumsy or difficult to train.

Stand by the dog's right side as in *Heel*. Face the same direction as the dog. Say *Sit* and praise the dog for going into the right position. Say *Stay*. Once again, praise the dog. You are now ready to begin the session. Continue to stand next to the dog. As in *Heel*, hold the leash with both hands. Let out enough leash so part of it barely scrapes the ground. Place the leash under your left shoe so it slides through the gap between the heel and the sole. Say *Down* in the stretched out tone of voice (see "Saying *Down* Properly," p. 235).

At the same time that you say the command *Down*, place

Place the leash under your left shoe so it slides through the gap between the heel and the sole. Say **Down.** At the same time, pull up on the leash in one continuous motion, sliding it through the arch of your shoe.

Photo by Pam Marks.

the dog into the Down position by pulling up on the leash in one continuous motion, sliding it through the arch of your shoe. The dog has no choice but to go into the Down position. Praise him just as he reaches the ground (see "Praise," p. 236). It is essential to repeat this method at least ten or fifteen times, until the dog does not resist being placed in the Down position. He may go Down without being placed in position at some point into the teaching of this method.

Skip the remaining methods and move directly to "Saying *Down* Properly" (p. 235).

6. The Foot-Leash Method

Do not use this method on any type of dogs except those with Strong-Willed or Easygoing or Sedate temperaments.

Stand by the dog's right side as in *Heel*. Face the same direction as the dog. Say *Sit*. Praise the dog for going into the Sit position. Say *Stay* and use the proper hand signal. Praise the dog. Continue to stand next to him. Hold the leash with both hands as you would for *Heel*. Create a small amount of slack in the leash. Say *Down* with an elongated, descending tone of voice as suggested in "Saying *Down* Properly" (p. 235).

As you say the command, lift your left foot above the leash and then bring it down on top of the leash where the clip connects to the collar. Apply pressure to the leash with your left foot as your voice starts going down. This will push the dog into the down position. Pull up on the leash as you press your foot down and get the leash to slide around on both sides of your shoe. Praise the dog with lots of enthusiasm once he gets to the ground. Never forget to

As you say the command **Down,** lift your left foot above the leash
and then bring it down on top of the leash where the clip connects to the collar.

Photo by Pam Marks.

praise the dog after each repetition (see "Praise," p. 236). Strong-Willed dogs who will not learn from any other method will definitely respond to this one. This is the best method, perhaps the only one, for a Strong-Willed dog that is also very big and powerful. It is essential to repeat this method ten or fifteen times, until the dog does not resist being placed in the Down position. After practice and repetitions the dog will probably begin to go into the Down position with just a verbal command.

Skip the remaining methods and move directly to "Saying *Down* Properly" (p. 235).

7. The Small-Dog Method

Humans often overwhelm small dogs. They look like threatening giants that could at any time become dangerous. You can avoid striking fear into the heart of a small dog by teaching this part of *Down* on a table. Using a tabletop is a good idea because the dog and his human appear to be at almost the same level: Your dog won't think that a human is towering over him, so he doesn't have to feel intimidated or frightened. What's also nice using a table that is that it's more comfortable for the person training the dog. Use a table for small dogs with the following temperaments: High-Energy; Shy; Strong-Willed; or Easygoing or Sedate.

Some small dogs can keep their balance on a smooth table surface and they can respond well to the Hand Method. However, a small dog may become shaky or upset when you pull his paws forward on a slick table and he begins to slide. You can help solve that problem by placing a rubber mat on the table surface. That will at least stop him from sliding. If he is still worried, use the Push Method or the Leg Method.

8. The Treat Method

If your dog will not respond to any of the other methods, you can always try to lure him into the Down position with a food treat he finds irresistible. Although I generally do not use food as a lasting training method, it *can* be useful for this command. When you use food as a lure it can be used with dogs of all temperaments, with the exception of those that become aggressive over their food.

Stand by the dog's right side as in *Heel*. Face the same direction as the dog. Say *Sit*. Praise the dog for going into the proper position. Say *Stay* and use the proper hand signal. Once again, praise the dog. Step off with your right foot and turn around to face him. You should be about eighteen inches in front. Continue to stand. Hang on to the leash with one hand. Give the dog about three feet of slackened leash. Say *Down* with the elongated, descending tone of voice (see "Saying *Down* Properly," p. 235).

Hold the food treat six to twelve inches in front of the dog's nose as you say *Down*. As your voice descends in tone, you must lure the dog into a Down position by lowering the food in your hand. Bring the food all the way down to the ground. The dog will probably follow the food treat into the Down position. If he does, give him your most enthusiastic praise and give him the food (see "Praise," on p. 236). Lift more food above his head and say *Sit*. Praise him. Say *Stay*, using the proper hand signal. Praise the dog again. It is essential to repeat this method until the dog wants to go into the Down position with the verbal command. The dog may begin to go down without the use of food at the end of this lesson.

Matty now has the Golden Retriever, Sparks, next to him. He is holding the leash and talking to Dan and Millie. He walks the

Hold the food treat six to twelve inches in front of the dog's nose as you say **Down.** Lure the dog into a Down position by lowering the food in your hand. Bring the food all the way down to the ground. The dog will probably follow the food treat into the Down position. Photos by Pam Marks.

dog back and forth, making turns, stopping, starting, and in general bonding with the dog.

"Okay, Sparks, what a good dog. Yes, you are. Let's show your mommy and daddy what you can do now. *Sit.*"

Sparks looks up at Matty and goes into a perfect Sit position.

"Good boy. *Stay.*"

Matty gives the dog the hand signal for Stay by placing his left hand in front of the dog's eyes for a second or two.

"Thank you."

He then kneels next to the dog and places the leash in his left hand. Matty takes hold of the dog's right leg just above the paw. He says the command word in a gentle but firm tone of voice.

"DOWWWWWwwwn."

As he begins to say the command in a slow, deliberate rhythm, he gently pulls the dog's right leg forward and just slightly to the side. This makes the dog start to move his body toward the ground. Matty does not stop saying the command word until Sparks has gotten all the way down to the ground.

"Oh, my, what a good boy you are. You did it! You did it just for me. Oh, Matty's proud."

Dan Deeter looks on with surprise.

Millie says, "Dan, look at that. Sparks finally went into the position. Did you notice how sensitive Matthew was as he got him into *Down?*"

"Hey, I can be sensitive. I can be sensitive if the damn dog'll let me. I'm very sensitive. Who's not sensitive? He just won't work for me, after all I've done for him, too."

"Sure, Hon. Maybe it's something we can work on. What's next, Matty?"

"Well, now that you have initiated the introductory training method for Sparks, you have to go on with the rest of the training elements for this command. It's important that you learn how to say *Down* for the rest of the teaching sessions."

Saying *Down* Properly

Does it matter how you say a command? Always. And it matters a great deal how you say this one. When you say *Down* to your dog the word will have meaning for the dog, and the very sound you make will help the dog understand what you want him to do. How can one word do that? Well, if you allow your voice to get lower and lower as you extend the word, it will suggest to anyone, including a dog, that what you want has something to do with lowering something. In this case it's the dog's body.

First, if you say the word as you normally would in other commands, it almost sounds like a punishment, especially if it is associated with this very difficult set of training lessons. Of course you still have to say it in a somewhat firm tone so you are the voice of authority that is necessary to command a dog into action. Second, if it still has a somewhat friendly sound, or is at least not unfriendly, it will reassure the dog that this is okay and that you love him. Third, by stretching out the word, and lowering your tone as you say the word, you are suggesting that he move downward. This is all supported of course by the teaching method and the hand signal. If you say the command word *Down* properly, it will definitely suggest downward motion to the dog. Your voice should drop as you continue to say the exaggerated version of *Down*. Do that and the dog will obey you and execute the command properly, assuming you have taught him what to do. Stretch out the middle part of the word so you do not finish saying it until the dog has reached the ground. As you start to stretch out the sound of "ow," allow your voice to lower so it follows the downward motion of the dog. The command will be like this: "DOWWWWWwwwn." Dogs have limited vocabularies, at least in English. But they connect with sounds they're given and will respond logically to them. It's like music, which is a language all of its own. "DOWWWWWwwwn" is a sound they remember all their lives, and so will you.

Leash Control

You can be sure your dog is going to get up and try to walk away if he decides he doesn't like what you are teaching. The proper use of the leash is your only way of controlling the situation and continuing the lesson. Do not give your dog any leash corrections while you are still teaching him the command. That can only interfere with the teaching process. Simply hold the dog in place with the leash extended above his head by about eighteen inches. You must keep it taut. If he actually gets up during the session, use the leash to place him in the *Sit* and *Sit-Stay* position again. Pull up on the leash and lower the dog by pushing down on his rear end. When initially teaching *Down* and *Down-Stay,* the leash should only be used to keep your dog in a sitting position as you slowly give the command and place him into a Down position.

Praise

Love, praise, and affection are the most important aspects of my approach to dog training. I doubt if I am the only one working this way, but I am very proud of the fact that I have been doing this since I started. As far as I'm concerned, praise is a key element in bonding with a dog and in training because it serves as a reward for doing the right thing.

Whenever the dog goes Down, or even heads in a downward direction, praise him to the sky and be generous about it, too. Let your cup overflow. But don't be surprised if your dog rolls over to his side once he's down. That's what going into a Down position may mean to him. Praise him anyway. Going Down on command is still going Down, and he deserves your praise and good will, even if he had to be placed in the proper position with one of the eight methods. What is essential at this stage of the teaching is that he absorbs the idea of the command. Even if he gets playful once he is Down, you should tolerate it, as long as you don't encourage this with rewards, laughter, or statements of approval, even if he does charm you. You can correct this behavior after the dog has learned the command. Remember, praise is the dog's reward for doing the right thing. It is the most useful way to communicate with your dog that he is a smart dog.

The Hand Signal at the Dog's Side

Once the dog begins to respond to the verbal command, it is time to teach him about the hand signal and how he is expected to respond to it. Start out at his side as described in all eight of the previous teaching methods. It's important to start that way because it allows you to control the dog more easily. By standing at the dog's side, you are able to work the leash more efficiently and with greater control. Even a dog that you would not consider aggressive may growl, snap, or try to bite you when you begin using or teaching the hand signal. Unless you have lived with the dog from the first day of his life, you do not entirely know what you are up against. If the dog has ever been hit, or for some other reason has a negative reaction to the command or the hand signal, he may surprise you with nasty behavior.

When starting this lesson, you should be at the dog's side, facing the same direction, but with one knee on the ground. Keep the leash in your right hand and keep your left hand free. Extend the leash to the right of the dog, in front of your body. There should be no slack. Let out only as much of the leash as necessary so it extends from the dog's collar to your right hand. Do not allow the dog to be playful at this time and do not allow him to jump on you. If he does, raise the leash so he has no room to do anything but sit. Say *Sit* and praise him for obeying the command. Return your right hand to its original position. Say *Stay* and, once again, praise the dog.

It is important for you to be in a happy frame of mind and not say or do anything brusque or severe. This is the crunch. Raise your left hand over the dog's head and just a bit to the right. Flatten it, close the fingers, and keep your palm side down toward the ground. Keep a taut leash with your right hand. Okay, this is crucial. Make sure your dog can see your left hand with his peripheral vision.

Say "*DOWWWWWwwwn*" as you lower your raised left hand toward the ground. On the way down, allow your hand to press the leash at the metal clip. This will push the dog to the ground as your hand presses hard against the leash. Once he has mastered the command, your dog will

Start at the dog's right side. Raise your left hand over the dog's

(continued on next page)

head and just a bit to the right. Say, **"DOWWWWWwwwn"** as you start lowering your hand toward the ground. On the way down, allow your hand to press the leash at the metal clip. This will push the dog to the ground as your hand presses hard against the leash.

Photos by Pam Marks.

always respond to your hand gesture as a command for him to go into a Down position. The reason for that association is that your left hand pushed him down as you said the verbal part of the command, *DOWWWWWwwwn*. Trust me, it won't take long for him to respond properly with no resistance. That's because he has already been taught the meaning of the vocal command "DOWWWWWwwwn" in one or more of the previous eight teaching methods and now knows what to do.

Bear in mind that it took the previous steps to achieve this. You may have to exert a lot of force to get the dog to move downward with the hand signal. You will be as tired as the dog at the end of this lesson. No matter how much the dog resists this part of the teaching, you must continue to push him down with your left hand on the leash and not worry about the collar tightening up. It will loosen once he goes down. As he gets down, praise him generously. Do not continue the lesson if he fights you hard on this. Stop, tell him he's a good boy, go into the Heel position, then *Sit* next *Stay,* and then start over. Start over from the very beginning of the command if he stubbornly resists this part of the command.

Do not lose your temper. Be very, very patient with a dog that resists the hand signal. You cannot teach a dog something like this with anger or intimidation. You must bring him around by reassuring him that you love him and that he always pleases you. Be persistent. Place yourself at the dog's side once again. Say *Sit* and praise him. Say *Stay* and praise him. Hold the leash tightly in your right hand and kneel down. Give the command "*DOWWWWWwwwn,*" and place your flattened left hand on top of the leash near the clip. Push the taut leash toward the ground as you did before. When, or if, the dog moves to the ground, be exuberant and praise him with many compliments like "Attaboy," "Good dog," and "You're terrific." Be very cheerful. Don't be afraid or inhibited to let the dog know how pleased you are. Learning *Down* is hard for most dogs and will take everything out of him pretty quickly. Remember, do not start another session in the same day for at least 4 hours.

Giving the Hand Signal While Kneeling in Front of the Dog

The next phase in teaching the hand signal involves standing or kneeling eighteen inches in front of the dog. He learned to respond to your downward moving hand from the side. Now he must learn to respond to it from the front. There is wisdom in this sequence. It was essential the dog saw your hand from the side at first. That's because there was no threat connected to your hand at your side. Having gone through the side portion of the lesson, it should now be easier for your dog to accept the hand signal from the front, and this is important. You should be able to give your dog the command *Down* with just the hand signal as you face him.

Stand next to the dog as in *Heel,* facing the same direction. Say *Sit* and praise him. Say *Stay* and once again praise him. Step in front of the dog. You may use the pivot technique from *Sit-Stay.* Hold the leash with your left hand and to your left side for control of the dog as you push him down. Get down on one knee. Lift your right hand up with your fingers closed and your palm down. Place it on top of the leash and push it to the ground. As you do this say,

"*DOWWWWWwwwn.*" Praise the dog lavishly when he gets to the ground in some form of the Down position.

Your dog may get playful, or even playfully aggressive, and try to nip your fingers. This is okay if he doesn't hurt you. He can be corrected when he knows the command perfectly. But if the dog wants to get away from you, or entangles himself around your legs, control him with the leash and start over by placing him in *Sit* and *Sit-Stay*. Do not praise him extravagantly after each repetition. Keep repeating this step until he performs it with no resistance. Do not go any farther than this in one day. Let the session end with success and praise and continue the next day. Do not tax the dog with demonstrations to your friends, relatives, or neighbors. The dog has worked hard, and he deserves to be left alone and allowed to sleep. Besides, he shouldn't be made to demonstrate anything until you are certain he has thoroughly imprinted it in his mind.

Down Without Kneeling

Repeat the previous two lessons concerning the hand signal. A major step forward now is teaching your dog to go into a Down position with a vocal command and a hand signal as you stand in front of him, no kneeling. Stand in front of the dog and move back about eighteen inches. Say *Sit* and praise the dog. Say *Stay* and once again praise him. Control your dog with the leash, which should be held in your left hand. Step forward quickly and tighten the leash by raising it above his head if he tries to get up. Give him the verbal correction *No,* immediately followed with praise. You may also use a leash correction if necessary because the dog has been taught the command and is familiar with it. Holding the leash above his head will hold him in place, if a correction is necessary. The dog has no choice but to sit and wait for you to correct him or redirect him. Get back to your position in front of him.

Allow three feet of the six-foot leash to go slack. Lift your right arm high and flatten your hand, put your fingers together, and turn your palm down facing the ground. Say "*DOWWWWWwwwn.*" At the same time lower your arm steadily. Lay your flat hand on top of the slackened leash, which should be angled off to your left. Considering all the training before, the dog should go into the Down position with no further effort on your part. He definitely should not have to be forced by the leash. Praise the dog with great enthusiasm, congratulate him, and make him feel special. Repeat this step ten times.

Down From a Greater Distance

Before starting again, allow your dog to rest, and then perform the same procedure, but do it from a greater distance. In the previous lesson, you stood approximately eighteen inches in front of the dog; now extend the distance to three feet. You are still close enough to correct the dog if he gets too playful or does not respond properly to the command. If he starts to move away or come forward, give him a leash correction and say *No* in a firm tone of voice. You may correct the dog now because he knows the command. All you are doing now is refining and sharpening the command. This cannot be considered teaching the basics anymore.

Lift your right arm, flatten your hand, put your fingers together, and turn your palm down facing the ground. Say "**DOWWWWW-wwwn.**" Lower your arm steadily. Lay your flat hand on top of the slackened leash. The dog should go into the Down position with no further effort on your part. He should not have to be forced in **Down** by the leash. Praise the dog lavishly.

Photos by Pam Marks.

Lift your right arm and flatten your hand, just as before. Say, "*DOWWWWWwwwn*" and lower your arm at a moderate, steady pace, with the palm of your hand facing the ground. There is one big difference now. As you lower your hand do not touch the leash. You must allow your hand to go past the leash without touching it. What you now have is the actual hand signal, as it will always be. After you lower your arm, return it to its natural position at the side of your body. As your arm comes down, the dog will assume that you are going to force him into position by pushing down on the leash. That will get him moving downward into the proper Down position in anticipation of being pushed down. Praise him generously and with excitement whenever he goes into the proper position. Repeat this lesson fifteen times. From here on, *Down* should come easily for him, and you. Just give him the command and the hand signal, which should never require anything more than lowering your raised arm.

The last phase of learning the hand signal is executing the procedure from six feet away—the full extend of the leash. Let's hope it isn't necessary to correct the dog at this point because it is more difficult to accomplish from this distance. Assuming your dog has learned everything up to this point and is able to carry it all out, he should be able to obey the command with just the hand signal or the voice command only, or both. In all dog training, practicing what the dog has learned is of vital importance. It is especially important with this command. When you practice, say "*DOWWWWWwwwn*" without the hand signal. Then repeat the procedure without the hand signal a number of times. Then switch to using the hand signal only, without the verbal command. This is tricky stuff and really tests how well the dog has learned this command. Use both hand signal and voice command in one final performance before ending the session. Be generous with your praise, which is very important as a motivator for your dog. Give him lots of enthusiastic praise every time he performs properly. It is worth repeating that you must never use your dog's name when you praise during the teaching of this command because it will make him get up and walk toward you, and that's the last thing you need in the middle of a teaching session.

It is possible that using the hand signal without the verbal command, or vice-versa, may confuse your dog. In that event, repeat the signal several times. Go back to giving the hand signal along with the voice command if he still doesn't respond properly. Then, try the hand signal only once again. Be consistent in the way you coordinate the lowering of your hand and your tone of voice. Always end a training session cheerfully. Wait for that time when the dog does the command well, praise him, and then stop.

Down for Dogs of Different Temperaments

If your dog has a High-Energy temperament, he is going to be a greater teaching challenge than most other types. He will move about in a restless but playful way. You must keep still no matter what, or you will not be able to teach him this command, which is difficult enough under the best of circumstances. Your dog is going to be like a shaken can of soda once it's snapped open. He is going to want to explode! Well, don't let him. Try exercising him before each session so you can use up some of his energy. Try running him as much as you can providing it doesn't make you too tired yourself to teach the lesson. You can always inhibit his restless movements by enclosing him between two chairs or some kind of arrangement on each side of him. Confine him after the exercise. Never give up. Insist that he behave himself and *Sit-Stay* for you. Be persistent, insistent, and patient.

When you teach this command, you are going to have to be fully energized and ready to rock and roll. How's your stamina? You're going to need it. Execute all motions and movements quickly and firmly no matter whether you are teaching from a kneeling or standing position.

Make sure your tone of voice is clear, loud enough, and firm. Voice corrections have to have a no-nonsense feeling to them, which means they should be on the firm side.

Strong leash corrections work best and are necessary at times. One strong correction is better than four mild ones.

Do not attempt to teach this command in a busy area, with interruptions or an audience. Choose a secluded area with no one present but the trainer and the dog. I think the privacy of your home, or backyard with no distractions, is the best place.

If your dog has a Shy temperament, stay aware of his emotional needs and limitations. Adjust your attitude at the start of the lesson with a timid or fear-ridden dog. If you are going to succeed in teaching this command, you must be as understanding and compassionate as possible, given the demands of this command. A Shy dog is very much like a frightened child. Make it your business to comfort the dog and to be very considerate.

Remember that the type of surface on which you train the dog can make it harder or easier for him as he moves up and down. He will be much more comfortable if you teach this command on grass, linoleum, or carpet. If you have a really frightened dog, let him sit and go Down on his favorite blanket or towel as you teach the command. If you want to succeed with a Shy dog, you must be patient, loving, and considerate.

Your movements and gestures must not be threatening in any way. Think about that before you start. Always kneel or sit next to, or in front of your Shy dog. I have had occasion to even lie down next to a Shy dog. Any unorthodox position is good if it is kind, thoughtful, and comforting in a way that helps a Shy dog deal with this command.

Your tone of voice should be gentle, casual, and very positive. Now is the time and place to be loving, and to express your devotion for your dog. Do not use voice corrections for a Shy dog. The teaching process incorporates enough of these anyway.

Use very few leash corrections, if any. If you do need to use a leash correction, then jerk the leash gently. The leash should be used more as a guide than as a correction tool in this command. I do not want the dog to think about the leash.

Make your Shy dog comfortable so the environment does not add any stress. Do not use a cement surface, or any other that is too hard, cold, or uncomfortable for the dog. Be considerate. When the weather gets hot, train the dog in a cool place. When the weather is cold, damp, wet, or icy, train the dog in a warm place.

If your dog has a Strong-Willed temperament, then you must think of him as a stubborn opponent! But try not to let this turn into a battle, because you will not win no matter which of the eight Down methods you use. Force will get you nowhere fast. Select one of the placing methods that show the dog what to do instead of those that force him into the position. Study all eight Down methods carefully to make an intelligent decision. You and the dog will be glad you chose carefully.

When teaching a Strong-Willed dog, it is useful to get on the dog's level by kneeling or bending down to him. Start the lessons on the side. This gives you more control over the dog, allowing the teaching process to be more fun.

Your tone of voice should be firm but not harsh. Your voice should communicate to the dog that although you are determined to get the job done, you are not going to be forceful. It is important that you do not overpower your dog with your voice. When you say the command words remember that they are not punishments, and you are not a drill sergeant.

Voice corrections have to be clearly spoken in a fast but authoritative manner. Do not yell *No*. It is easy to have your corrections send no-nonsense message without being too loud or sounding angry.

When giving leash corrections, keep control of the leash and be firm. You must give strong corrections if they are needed. One strong correction is far more effective than four mild ones in a row.

A Strong-Willed dog should be trained in a quiet area such as your backyard or a room in your home. Dogs of this temperament require training in privacy.

If your dog has an Easygoing or Sedate temperament, there is not much to worry about. Training this type of dog for *Down* is no big deal. A dog of this temperament will actually lie down for you if you ask. It is important to understand the difference though between a dog's learning the command, or resting because he's bored or tired. If you're smart, you will make the dog's easygoing nature work for you by continually repeating the commands so he will lie down each time you tell him to.

You should kneel down beside the dog when you train him. Everything else will probably fall into place quite easily as you teach the procedures and methods.

A soft tone of voice is best when the dog is in the learning phase. Put more energy into your voice if the dog becomes detached to what you are teaching. Do not allow your dog to become bored, lazy, or tired.

When you use voice corrections, it may be necessary to be firm when the dog does not pay attention. He may be too easygoing.

Leash corrections help to guide the dog through the various lessons. In the beginning, dogs of this temperament often try to roll over on their back. You should accept this behavior only in the beginning, but if he continues to lie down during the teaching, you must use leash corrections to stop it.

You may train an Easygoing or Sedate dog anywhere. Wherever you train him will be just fine. Use a place that is easy for you.

If your dog has an Aggressive temperament, it is very possible that you will get bitten when teaching *Down*. Your dog's age, as well as which of the Down teaching methods you use, are key issues. Almost all the teaching methods are acceptable for Aggressive dogs under ten months of age. If your dog is over ten months of age, use the food method, or the foot method ONLY. Do not teach this command yourself if your dog has ever bitten anyone. Talk to a professional dog trainer.

Your body language requires that your gestures and movements are strictly nonthreatening. Never stare directly in the eyes of an Aggressive dog over ten months old. In dog behavior, a direct stare into his eyes indicates a challenge to the animal's top dog status, and could trigger aggressive behavior. Never stand directly over an Aggressive dog. Kneel down alongside him. Another important factor is the dog's age. If your Aggressive dog is under ten months of age, he is going to be less dangerous than if he is over ten months of age. You must be careful. Do not assume that you know your dog. In the right circumstances, any Aggressive dog is capable of becoming threatening.

The tone of voice you use depends on the dog's age, and if he is Dominant-Aggressive or Fear-Aggressive. Dominant-Aggressive puppies between the ages of seven weeks and six months should be commanded and corrected with a firm tone of voice. Do not be harsh, however. Dominant-Aggressive dogs between six and ten months of age require an authoritative, demanding tone of voice. Fear-Aggressive puppies between the ages of seven weeks and six months require a soft tone of voice. Even so, you must be firm enough to make a correction effective. Use a firm tone of voice for Fear-Aggressive dogs between six and ten months of age. But do not be harsh. Talk to a professional dog trainer about help for an aggressive dog past ten months of age.

Voice corrections for dogs of this temperament are not usually effective unless they are accompanied by a leash correction at the same time. Seriously aggressive dogs are not usually impressed with voice corrections. That is why it is a good idea to always have an Aggressive dog on a leash for training. Do not forget to follow every correction with generous praise for responding properly to the correction.

Before you use leash corrections on a dog with an Aggressive temperament, you must think about the dog's age, size, and degree of aggressiveness. Ask yourself if the dog is a bully. Does he growl, snarl, or curl his lip? When a puppy is between the ages of seven weeks and six months, he should be corrected with quick, firm leash jerks that are not too hard. Correct a dog between six and ten months of age with quick, firm jerks. It may be necessary to give slightly harder jerks at that age, depending on how aggressive he is.

Correct aggressive behavior quickly to have any hope of stopping it. You must repeat the corrections until the dog stops behaving aggressively. You should be able to see excellent results by administering corrections every time they are needed, unless the dog is severely aggressive. It is important to understand that it is only safe to correct an Aggressive dog until he is ten months old. Dogs older than that can be too dangerous for anyone other than a professional dog trainer.

Train an aggressive dog in private. Avoid distractions, such as dogs, kids, or spectators. Use your home or your backyard.

How to Teach Your Dog *Down-Stay*

A dog in *Down-Stay* has assumed the Down position on the ground and remains there, on command, until he is released by verbal command. While he is on the ground his head should remain erect and he should be looking straight ahead. His front legs extend forward and his hind legs are relaxed as they rest on one or both haunches. He must stay alert until you release him if he is to remain in that position for three to five minutes. He may make himself comfortable and even go to sleep if he is to remain in *Down-Stay* for longer than five minutes.

I have to assume that the dog has learned *Sit-Stay*. If that is the case, then you must go back to *Sit-Stay* and use the same techniques for *Down-Stay* with the following exceptions.

Wherever it instructs you to place the dog in *Sit*, substitute *Down* for that command. After placing your dog in *Down*, give the command *Stay* in a firm tone of voice. *Stay* is not a command involving forward motion, so you must not use the dog's name before or after giving a command or correction.

When you give the command *Stay*, flatten your left hand with your fingers close together as though you were swimming and place it in front of the dog's eyes. Your hand should not be closer than four inches from his eyes. Give the hand signal at the same time you say the voice command. The hand signal is a quick gesture that is meant to block the dog's vision for a split second, just long enough to know it happened. If your dog knows *Sit-Stay*, all the rest should fall neatly into place. If he does not respond properly, then review Chapter Six, "*Stay* a While," and start over but substitute *Down* for *Sit.*

"Matty, is there some secret you can teach us to make this command a little easier to teach?" asked Dan.

"There is, Dan. First, you have to be on good terms with your dog. That means bonding. Then you have to figure out what kind of dog you have so you can adjust the training methods and techniques to your dog's temperament. As far as teaching *Down* is concerned, if you remember, I used the Dog's Leg Method for Sparks. But even more important than that choice was that I was kneeling next to the dog rather than standing over him, and when I pulled his leg out, I did it without warning. It surprised him and he started to go down before he had a chance to think about it and resist me. One of the mistakes you made, Dan, was to stand up in the middle of teaching the command."

"Oh, yeah. That's right, I did. And the minute I stood up, so did Sparks."

"Right. And once I got him down, I rubbed his belly and played with him for just a bit."

"But Matty, that means he won't be down in the proper position."

"Well, at that point it doesn't matter. With a hard case like Sparks the most important thing is to just get him to go down and stay down for a short while. Once you get him down you can reposition him. Look, this is the hardest command to teach with the greatest reward to offer. Being able to put your dog in the Down position for any

After placing your dog in **Down,** say **Stay.** Flatten your left hand and close your fingers as though you were swimming. Place your hand in front of the dog's eyes not closer than four inches. Make a pivotal turn so you face the dog. Keep the leash taut above his head. Stand in front of the dog for about 30 seconds. As you back away from the dog, slide the leash through your right hand as you hold firmly in the left so the leash gets longer as you move backward. (See Chapter Six and apply details of **Sit-Stay** for **Down-Stay.**)

Photos by Pam Marks.

length of time has so many benefits I can't begin to list them. So go back and start over."

"Start over? But you just taught the command to Sparks."

"Dan, you and Millie have to do the rest. I only did the introductory method. You still have all the rest to do."

"Oh, no," said Dan

Matty smiles.

"Bargain basement is next. Going Down."

Eight
Come to Me, My Melancholy Baby

Come When Called

The charcoal grill sizzles and smokes as tiny beads of steak juice drizzle on the hot coals from the sirloins which are ready to be turned. Just three minutes more to medium-rare. The ears of corn are light amber and a foil packet of buttered carrots bubble over the grill. The smell of the wet mesquite chips burning on the charcoal smells like August in Yellowstone. Suddenly your beeper goes off and continues to nag but before you have a chance to look at it your cell phone rings. Not too far from your backyard you hear a horn honking furiously and then two other horns and then the squealing of brakes.

One of your guests shouts out to you, "Billy, is your dog a large Dalmatian with a red collar? There's one out in the middle of the road and he's going to get hit unless someone gets him out of there."

So you run to the road and spot your dog. Sure enough

it's Rex looking bewildered as he stands on the white line between both lanes.

Someone yells from the house, "Billy, the steaks are burning."

The cell phone rings again but you don't answer it. The beeper goes off, too. You look both ways and there's traffic coming from each direction. You look at your beloved dog and gasp. He is motionless with fear. After a minute or two the road empties. There isn't a car or truck coming from either direction for at least a block. What will you do? What *will* you do?

I guess you have no choice but to run out in the middle of the road, grab your dog by the collar, and pray the oncoming traffic will stop for both of you. You could do that unless, of course, good old Rex runs from you as you try to get to him. Whenever you ran at him in the past he considered it a game and ran around in circles hoping you'd chase him. That would be deadly now.

Of course, had you taught him the command *Come When Called* you could stay where you are and run down the proper sequence of commands that would save his life. That ending would go like this:

"Sit! Good boy. Stay! Good boy."

Look at each direction of the road to be sure there is no car traffic and wait for it to clear.

"Okay, Rex Come!"

Good old Rex, who has obeyed all of your commands and who is totally focused on you, makes a fast dash across the road and runs right up to you. As he approaches, he immediately goes into a perfect Sit position and looks up at you, waiting for your praise, which you give him instantly, after you hug him and thank your lucky stars for Come When Called.

Of course, the carrots have dried out, the ears of corn have turned black, and I hope you like your sirloin fried like shoe leather. Hey, you haven't checked your beeper and you have no idea who called on the cell phone. Nevertheless, the evening was a great success. Your dog is still among the living.

"Come on, Rex. Have some steak. What? You don't like it well-done either?"

Now you have to work on confining Rex so he doesn't get loose in the first place.

I hope you understand the value of *Come When Called.* Not every situation will be life or death, but being able to call your dog to you from a distance, even though he is off-leash, is every dog owner's fantasy—and life saver. I have to tell you, though, dogs do not normally do that unless you teach them *Come When Called.* (I have to say that I do not encourage anyone to allow their dog to run around free, off-leash. It is too dangerous. Thousands of dogs are lost every year in auto accidents. Very few dogs are reliable enough that they can be trusted to respond properly to street and road traffic one hundred percent of the time. They have to be reliable one hundred percent of the time because you are only one mistake away from tragedy.)

The command *Come When Called* can be extremely useful in many ordinary situations that are not life-and-death but important anyway. Such was the case when I taped a segment for my PBS special *Woof! Woof!!* at the beautiful Hollywood home of TV star JoMarie Payton-Noble, the tough, funny, lovable mom in the show *Family Matters.* That's the one with Urkle as the next-door neighbor. We started out dealing with a housebreaking problem with Champ, her male Yorkshire terrier. But guess what? In order to deal with the dog's housebreaking problem, we had to get the dog to come to us. We ended up dealing with Champ's refusal to *Come When Called.* Sometimes, to solve one dog problem, you must first deal with another. I went inside their gorgeous home to find out if we were dealing with a Champ problem or a JoMarie problem. Because of the subject of this chapter, I am going to skip the housebreaking part of that episode and get right to the *Come When Called* part.

The scene opened with JoMarie's husband, Rodney, and their daughter, Chantell, running up and down the carpeted stairs trying to get hold of Champ so we could give him a bit of training. They ran up and down the stairs after that mighty little terrier who wasn't about to let himself get caught.

"Champola. Come Champ. Git 'em Chantell," yelled JoMarie from the bottom of the staircase as both Rodney and Chantell were trying to get ahold of the little dog.

Matty looks into the camera.

"I'm calling and he's not coming. That's the big problem with Champ. They say he never comes when they call him. So we're going to talk to them again and find out what the problem is."

JoMarie yells, "Champ. Get down here. Champ!"

"Let's talk about this. What happens?" asked Matty.

JoMarie is leaning against the bottom banister holding her head up with one hand. She looks ready to throw in the towel.

"Rodney calls him and sometimes he'll come. Sometimes! He's spoiled, and I am not the one who does it. Champ is total madness. Git 'em Chantell. Because he's so small he gets under the tables and chairs and it's hard to catch him."

JoMarie and Rodney are now on their knees trying to get the Yorkie out from under the dining-room table.

"Champ! See him? Look at him. Come here. He's all over. Champ. Come on, Champ. Now he's gone into the kitchen. Oh!"

Matty smiles and tries to comfort her.

"Why doesn't he come to you? You said you think he knows what you mean when he doesn't come. Why?" asked Matty.

She responds with an angry sigh, "He's a hard-headed dawg."

"Have you ever called him by his name and then said '*No.* Champ what did you do? Champ, *bad* dog. Champ, come here' and then said *No* in a harsh tone," probed Matty.

JoMarie answered thoughtfully, "I think sometimes we have. I know *I* have."

"Have you ever called him over and said 'Champ, what did you do' for the housebreaking, like he made a housebreaking mistake? Did you ever call him and say 'What did you do, Champ, bad dog?'"

"Yeah. I *have* said 'Why have you done that?' Oh, yeah."

Matty tries to explain their mistake to JoMarie and Rodney as all three sit at the edge of the swimming pool. Rodney is holding Champ and stroking him.

"Okay. So, poor Champ hears his name: 'Champ, No! Champ, get in here! Champ, I'm going to show you what you've done wrong. Champ, Champ, and Champ!' Right? Is that true?"

She nods as if confessing and says, "Yes. So true."

"So what do you think Champ thinks about his name? It's a negative, right?"

"Yeah."

"So what you have to learn from this is if you use his name with a negative, like Champ, no, Champ what did you do? Champ, bad dog he won't come to you, right?"

"Yeah, yeah. *That* makes a lot of sense."

"Okay. And Champ should want to come to you because he loves you. Which he does. But he also says to himself, well what's in it for me? If I said to you, JoMarie, get in here, it ain't happy birthday, right?"

"Absolutely."

"That's right. So that's what Champ hears and is thinking. And remember, dogs hear a lot better than we do. So the louder you yell, the worse it is. All right? You don't want to scare Champ. You don't want to yell at him. We're talking about love, praise, and affection. Also, when you want to say *Come,* instead of saying 'Champ, come,' say, '*Okay*, Champ, *Come,*' and make your voice very high. Go ahead, let me hear you do this."

She makes a sincere but gruff effort.

"Come on Champie. Come on Champie."

The Yorkie takes one look at her, turns around, and runs out of sight around the other side of the large house.

"Boy, look how fast he's running to you. You sound like you're saying, 'I'll kill you if you don't get over here,' right?"

"No, not really, because I love him. I do love him. I just want him to behave and obey."

"Well you've got to be nice to him and say, 'Come on Champie (*in the Uncle Matty high-pitch voice*). Come on Champie. Come on, do this.'"

She shouts, "Come on Champie. Well he's so far away now that…"

"He'll hear you."

"No, he'll hear me if I say his name the way I usually do."

"Go ahead, let me hear you say it."

"Chaaaamp," she says in her very deep, affectionate but gruff-sounding voice, the one we have heard her use as the mother on her TV show. "Chaaaaaamp!"

Matty shakes his head and laughs as the little dog runs away again.

"Man, I wouldn't come to that. Go like this..." *Matty consoles her and uses his Uncle Matty falsetto again.* "JoMarie's proud! Champ."

JoMarie musters all her acting ability and tries to produce Uncle Matty's falsetto sound.

"Come on. Come on, Champie."

The little dog runs back to them as they sit on the edge of the pool. Champ runs right past JoMarie and Rodney and jumps into Matty's lap. JoMarie frowns.

"He went to you!"

Matty laughs and lifts the dog up and hugs him as the little dog licks his face.

"Oh, you came to Matty. You came to Matty. So you know what the secret is." *Matty speaks in his Uncle Matty falsetto voice,* "Matty's proud. Champ's the best."

Come When Called is an important command and offers a great deal of satisfaction to the pet owner because when you really need it nothing else will do. Getting your dog to respond properly during dire circumstances requires a good bit of self-control on your part. You must not show any sign of panic because the essence of the command is to sound upbeat and cheerful, as though nothing is wrong. A dog will not come to you unless he thinks it is going to be a pleasant experience. What person or animal in his right mind would go to you if he thought you were going to smack him or holler at him? Actually, I do know a few people who would, but that's a whole other book.

The *Come When Called* command requires that you say *Okay* first, just to get the dog's attention with a happy sound. After *Okay,* say the dog's name because by now he should be associating that with forward motion. Next, say *Come.* That is the entire verbal command. Saying any more than that just adds confusion, uncertainty, and a possible lack of response from the dog. So the whole thing together is: *Okay,* Champ, *Come.*

Allowing your dog to run around off-leash is, in my opinion, a very dangerous thing to do. It doesn't matter whether you live with a grown dog or a puppy, whether you live in the city, the suburbs, or in a rural area. A dog loose on his own is always in danger of being hit by traffic. **PLEASE** consider this before using *Come When Called* outdoors, where it's hard to be safe. It could result in the death of your animal. However, if you make use of this command indoors, or in a confined outdoor area, it is both practical and convenient. The purpose of the command is obviously to get the dog to come to you. This command can easily be taught indoors. If you decide to teach it outdoors, **I BEG YOU** to use a fenced backyard or an out-of-the-way local park.

When the command is performed properly, you must use a precise verbal command as well as a hand signal. These must be administered correctly so the dog stops what he is doing, runs to you, and places himself in a Sit position in front of you. The dog must be able to do this no matter how many distractions there are, and what they may be.

Unless you know the teaching technique, it is almost impossible to get a dog to do this, despite the fact that this command is what dog owners most desire. Executing this command is very demanding for a dog, and only animals that have been diligently trained will do it. A dog's life often does not have many responsibilities attached to it, other than to be a good companion and loving friend. That's why a good bit of a dog's life involves sleeping, playing, and following you around in addition to looking into anything and everything that strikes his curiosity. *Come When Called* requires that a dog be able to shift his focus instantly to you, and use all his concentration to obey you. There is not much of a challenge to this command when it is given indoors. But if you give it outdoors, you will be competing with sights; smells; other dogs; children; people; moving objects; and noises—all of which are very interesting indeed. Resisting all that, and meeting the demands of the command is a major accomplishment for any dog and his trainer.

If you want this command to work and have your dog respond properly, then NEVER call him to you to reprimand him, punish him, holler at him, or express your dissatisfaction with anything he has done. If you use his name or the command *Come When Called* and then correct or punish him, he will never come to you again.

Never call your dog to you with this command and say, "Bad dog! What did you do? Never, never do that again!" And if you actually hit your dog, forget using the command ever again, because he would have to develop amnesia before he would come to you again after you hit him. Praise your dog every time he obeys a command. If he comes to you after you call him, it is wrong to holler at him. If you use his name when correcting him, you will give him unpleasant associations with his own name, and that has many consequences. It is foolish to think that a dog will run to you so he can get hollered at or punished. That doesn't mean you cannot correct him for disobedience or misbehavior. But you must go to him to do that, rather than call him to you.

A dog should feel that coming to you is a good thing. You must do this with a very happy tone of voice, as well as a positive attitude. Give the dog a lot of praise every time he obeys, or comes to you. If you do this on a regular basis, your dog will always come to you when called.

Your dog should be completely responsive to this command the moment you give it. He must never be unsure of what to do, because that's a habit that could cost him his life. He should respond immediately. Reward him with heaps of praise for obeying instantly. Establish that you always demand that he come to you the first time you say the command. Remember—it could be a lifesaver.

How to Teach Your Dog the Command *Come When Called* On-Leash

It does not matter whether you begin teaching this command indoors or out. Either way it requires a six-foot leather leash and a metal training collar. Work in an area that has few distractions. A place with moderate activity or noise is acceptable. Always start by having your dog run through all the commands he knows up to this point. Have him do *Heel, Sit, Sit-Stay, Down,* and *Down-Stay.* Then say *Sit.* Praise the dog. Say *Stay* and praise him again. Face the dog and begin the lesson.

Stand directly in front of your dog, about five and a half feet away. Hold the leash in your left hand with your thumb in the loop, allowing just a little slack so the dog will not accidentally be pulled toward you. If the leash is pulled at all, the dog will leave his position. Hold the leash slightly above your waist. This will give you optimum control over the animal.

The lesson begins with the verbal command, which must be given with great joy and enthusiasm. The sound of your voice should tell the dog that something fun is about to happen. *Come When Called* is an action command involving forward motion and requires the dog's name to be used before the word *Come*. In this case, however, you must use something that comes before the dog's name. Use the word *Okay* before saying the dog's name. The entire verbal command is *Okay*, Champ, *Come!* You say *Okay* before your pet's name is to insure an upbeat sound that gets the dog's attention. From a distance, a command that just uses his name might sound like you are going to correct him because you had to raise your voice. But if you say *Okay*, in a high-pitched, happy tone of voice, it makes it clear to the dog that this is a good thing. *Okay* is hard to say in a bad way.

When you say the full verbal command, it is important to emphasize the word *Okay*. Eliminate any harshness from your voice and sound as affectionate as possible. Once the dog learns the command, he should start moving toward you when he hears *Okay*, because it tends to be the most prominent part of the phrase, *Okay*, Champ, *Come*. This should be the only way that you ever call the dog to you. Make it clear to everyone in the family and be consistent. It is very important. Try calling the dog in this manner and see if he comes to you. If he does, delight him with praise. If he doesn't, do not correct him. Keep calling the dog with the verbal command until he finally comes to you. It may only take a short while. It is not important at this point that he sits once he gets to you. If he jumps on you the first few times, it's understandable and acceptable, for now. Remember that I never correct a dog while he is being taught something new. I do not want him to associate coming to me with a correction. If he does, then he will never obey the command. You can always correct him some other time, once he has learned the command.

Gently Pull the Leash

Now that the dog moves toward you on the verbal command it is time to reinforce his understanding. Gently pull on the leash as you say *Okay*. This is how it should work: *Okay* (gently pull the leash), Champ, *Come*. Once the dog comes to you, praise him. "Good boy! What a good dog!" Never forget the praise. The quality of the dog's learning will depend on the quality of your praise. Do not be inhibited. When you are outdoors you may have to compete with street sounds; kids at play; stray dogs; birds; and anything else that moves or makes noise. Praise will win out over all of it if you give it enthusiastically.

Teaching the Hand Signal

The verbal command is always accompanied by a hand signal. The hand signal helps eliminate any confusion for the dog if he is called from a distance. The hand signal is based on the very common gesture that is used to summon someone from a long way off. The right arm leaves its hanging position at the side of the body and is raised in a turning, leftward motion as though it were wrapping around a large object. The entire command for the purpose of this lesson goes like this: *Okay* (pull the leash with your left hand, raise your right arm and swing it around to your left side, complete the gesture and return your arm to its natural position), Champ, *Come*. Praise the dog.

The Sit Position

Stand in front of the dog at a distance of almost six feet. Say *Sit*. Praise the dog. Say *Stay* and once again praise the dog. Give the verbal command, *Okay* (give the hand signal and pull the leash), Champ, *Come*. Immediately, start pulling the leash toward you like a fishing line, using both hands in a hand-over-hand method. Do this until the line is mostly taken up. As the dog gets to your feet, give him the command *Sit*, and raise the leash twelve inches above his head, holding it with both hands. Keep the leash taut so he has no choice but to obey your command and sit. Heap tons of praise on him so he begins to do it on his own, if only to be praised.

Once again, the sequence is: *Okay* (tug the leash with your left hand and swing your right hand around, making a complete gesture), Champ, *Come*. Then pull in the leash, using both hands. "Good boy, good boy." By now you have pulled him gently to your feet. Raise the leash with both hands. "*Sit!* Good boy. That's a good boy."

It is very impressive when a dog comes to you and immediately sits. But having the dog go into the Sit position after he comes to you has nothing to do with impressing anyone. If the dog is a distance away, he responds to your command by running. If he has enough distance, he can

Place your dog in Sit and Sit-Stay. Back away from him slowly until you reach about six feet. Say "**Okay**, Champ, **Come**." Emphasize the word **Okay**. Start pulling the leash toward you. As the dog gets to your feet, say **Sit**, and raise the leash twelve inches

above the dog's head, and keep it taut so that he has no choice but to obey your command and sit. Praise the dog generously.

Photos by Jonathan Alcorn/Zuma.

build up his speed to almost forty miles an hour depending on the breed/size of the dog. If he crashes into you, it will knock you down. He may also not be able to stop and will run past you. Once he has been taught to sit after responding to *Come When Called* he will automatically pace himself so he begins to slow down before he gets to you. These techniques should be repeated at least fifteen times each, or until the dog performs properly. For safety reasons, you must use the leash at all times. Once the dog is performing the command properly, you may increase the distance for him by backing away as he walks toward you. Use verbal praise as you back away. Praise holds his attention and motivates him for future commands. "*Okay*, Champ, *Come*. Good boy." Remember that all of this is done on-leash. At no time should you try it without the leash. The most important reason is safety. But another reason is control, so your dog can be guided if he starts veering left or right.

Remember, never say the *Come When Called* command in a harsh tone of voice and never reprimand the dog after he has obeyed the command. This rule applies in your home, outdoors, and during training sessions. If the dog chews something in the living room and you call him in from the kitchen to scold or correct him, you will be destroying the value of this command.

Come *When* Called for Dogs of Different Temperaments

If your dog has a High-Energy temperament, he is going to run around and move everywhere except where you want him to be. Be ready for this by offering lavish praise and a general sense of excitement about what you are about to do. You want to keep him focused on you so he will come to you as you progress with the teaching of this command, despite his desire to run around. Direct his energy in such a way that he will love coming to you, and that means praising him to the sky. All training sessions should be this way.

It is doubly important with dogs of this temperament never to call him to you in anger, or with any possible threat. Do not use his name when you're correcting him or reprimanding him because his name is an important part of the *Come When Called* command. A dog's name must always be associated with something positive. When he comes to you in response to the command, give him a great deal of verbal recognition. Never chase him. Never call him to you and then punish.

No special body language is called for. You just have to stand there and use the leash properly. A High-Energy dog will be very energized and you will have to be much calmer than your pet.

Your tone of voice should sound happy but determined. The dog should understand from the tone of your voice that you are in control and demanding. He should also understand that you are a fountain of spoken compliments, which are his rewards.

When it becomes necessary and you must use voice corrections, make them loud enough to be effective, and quick enough so he understands you are not playing around.

Your leash corrections should communicate to the dog that he must calm down and listen to you, and then obey your commands. Leash corrections for dogs of this temperament should be strong when given.

Train the dog in a quiet, secluded location. This will help him concentrate and keep his mind on what you are teaching him. Do not allow any distractions to interrupt the training or break his concentration.

If your dog has a Shy temperament, *Come When Called* is going to be a bit more difficult for him than other kinds of dogs. But keep in mind that most dogs, whether they are shy or not, will not come to you when you call them if they haven't been completely trained to do it. Your dog is not going to stop whatever he is doing just to respond to your call, and it is a fantasy to think he will. Some dogs will run to you when you call them if they have been conditioned to associate your call with being fed. Shy dogs have the most difficult time with this command. They need a lot of encouragement and persuasion.

Your Shy dog needs you to communicate an enthusiastic, happy attitude when you call him. If you can do that, he will come to you. It is especially important for a dog with a Shy temperament that you never display or reveal anger, or even mild disapproval, during the teaching of this command. As you already know, the dog's name is part of the spoken command phrase, and it must always be the equivalent to something nice. Never, never use your dog's name when correcting him. Do not chase him ever, not even as a game. Never call him to you to punish or scold. Encourage your Shy dog with heaps of enthusiastic praise. Follow these suggestions and you will succeed with this command.

When you are training a Shy dog, your body language must indicate that you are upbeat and enthusiastic. Move around energetically. Swing your arms. Run backward. Have a good time. Energize your dog and get him pleasantly involved with the teaching process. Do not make any motions that can be misinterpreted by the dog as unsafe or intimidating. Make the session fun.

Your voice should be full of life and happy energy.

Do not give Shy dogs voice corrections. Use praise instead of corrections if something goes wrong. Give few, if any, leash corrections. Use the leash as a guide rather than as a tool.

Train the Shy dog at home. Take advantage of the privacy available there, or in your backyard. Shy dogs cannot work if there are distractions or spectators.

If your dog has a Strong-Willed temperament and you give him the chance, he will take advantage of you. But you mustn't lose your patience. Take charge and stay in charge. A dog of this kind, a stubborn dog, is going to go as far as he can before you come down on him. You must out think, out wait, and outsmart a dog with a Strong-Willed temperament. Even so, do not be harsh in your attitude or manner. Just be more stubborn than your dog! A Strong-willed Dog can be taught to respond to this command very well, but it takes patience and a strong will of your own, one that matches your stubborn dog.

Your chances of succeeding with this command are enhanced one hundred percent if you never call your dog to you in anger. Do not use the dog's name in any negative way. Your dog's name is an important part of the *Come When Called* command, and it must always have a positive feeling connected to it. When a Strong-Willed dog comes to you, praise him lavishly. Never chase him and never call him to you to correct him.

Your body language for a dog of this temperament involves authority and self-assurance. This can be conveyed if you stand straight and tall and move about freely and without constraint.

Your tone of voice should be firm and indicate that you are very much in charge. Maintain a no-nonsense attitude.

Your voice corrections should be clear; precise; obvious; and consistent.

Leash corrections require a quick, firm jerk of the leash. The correction is more effective with dogs of this temperament with one really firm jerk rather than a number of mild ones.

Train the dog in a quiet area with no distractions.

If your dog has an Easygoing or Sedate temperament, he will come to you in his own sweet time during the teaching process. You must be patient or you will be very discouraged. Listen to a Walkman, have a snack, read a magazine. Whatever it takes, have faith that the dog will eventually learn the command and actually respond properly to it. You have no choice with an Easygoing or Sedate dog but to accept the fact that he will learn the command in his own time.

Whenever you teach or use this command, never call your dog to you in anger or with any threat. Do not use his name when you correct him. His name is an important part of the *Come When Called* command and must always be a pleasant thing in his mind. Praise him lavishly when he comes to you. Never chase him and never call him to you to correct him.

Your body language must indicate that you are upbeat and enthusiastic about teaching this command. Move energetically. Swing your arms. Run backward. Have a good time. Energize your dog and get him pleasantly involved with the teaching process. Make the session fun. The idea is to motivate an Easygoing dog with enthusiasm.

Use a happy tone of voice that rewards the dog with praise and approval.

If you use voice corrections, make them firm and definite whenever the dog fails to pay attention. Do not be harsh. Do not confuse firmness with harshness.

Use firm leash corrections when necessary. If your dog loses interest or allows himself to become bored, give him a gentle leash correction and try running backward as you pull him toward you. Make a game out of it. Do anything pleasant that energizes the dog and gets him back into the session. Not only will the dog learn to come to you, he may also start enjoying the training sessions.

Train a dog of this temperament in any location you find comfortable. Training an Easygoing or Sedate dog in a place with distractions actually helps him learn the command. The sights and smells of new places and different people may involve the dog with the teaching process.

If your dog has an Aggressive temperament, chances are he is going to challenge you when you try to teach this command. If that happens, try doing the unexpected. Run backward or toss a ball, a stick, or toy—or anything that says "fun." Use your imagination. Go with the idea that you want to get the dog to come to you and you must use anything you can to achieve that in the beginning.

If you want to successfully teach this command to your Aggressive dog, then you must never call him to you in anger or with any implied threat. Do not use his name when you correct him, because his name is an important part of the *Come When Called* command and must always be connected to something good. Praise your Aggressive dog generously when he comes to you. You must never chase him, and never call him to you to correct or punish him.

Do not use any body language that could be interpreted by the dog as threatening. Run backwards, flail your arms in fun, bend down, do anything with your body in ways that will motivate an Aggressive dog. Lighten him up.

Your tone of voice should be soft; gentle; affectionate; and persuasive.

When giving voice corrections, use *No* as a correction and be firm without being threatening.

When giving leash corrections, use a medium to firm jerk, depending on the dog's size, age, and level of aggressiveness.

Train an aggressive dog in the privacy of your home or backyard. Do not allow any spectators to watch, and avoid distractions.

You know, I've been training dogs for more than thirty years, and I've stuck to one philosophy: Train the dog from the dog's point of view, which means understanding your dog. So if you are the teacher and the dog is the student, then patience comes into it, and love comes into it, and understanding comes into it. And don't we all want that? That's the secret. And then, of course, using love, praise, and affection comes into it. We all want that, too. So give it to your best friend. I promise you, he'll love you for it. I'll see you on television.

About the Authors

Mordecai Siegal is the author of twenty-four books about dogs, cats, and horses. As a writer specializing in pets, he frequently appears on radio and television and at speaking engagements. He is the president of the Dog Writers Association of America. *The Ultimate Guide to Dog Training* is the eighth Siegal-Margolis book, the result of an enduring collaboration. He lives in New York City.

Matthew Margolis, "Uncle Matty," is the engaging host of his own TV series, *Woof! It's a Dog's Life with Matthew Margolis,* presented on PBS by WGBH, Boston and aired on PBS stations throughout the United States. The series stems from his two earlier PBS specials, *Woof! A Guide to Dog Training* and *Woof! Woof! Uncle Matty's Guide to Dog Training.* He is the resident pet expert for *Good Morning America* and is often seen on ABC's *20/20.* He is the recipient of the Communicator of the Year Award from the Dog Writers Association of America and runs the National Institute of Dog Training in Los Angeles, the largest dog-training facility in the United States.